PIRATES

THE
TRYALS
OF
Captain John Rackam,
AND OTHER
PIRATES, *Viz.*

Geroge Fetherston,	Noah Harwood,
Richard Corner,	James Dobbins,
John Davies,	Patrick Carty,
John Howell,	Thomas Earl,
Tho. Bourn, *alias* Brown,	John Fenwick, *al'* Fenis

Who were all Condemn'd for PIRACY, *at the Town of* St. Jago de la Vega, *in the Island of* JAMAICA, *on Wednesday and Thursday the Sixteenth and Seventeenth Days of* November 1720.

AS ALSO, THE

TRYALS *of* Mary Read *and* Anne Bonny, *alias* Bonn, *on Monday the* 28th *Day of the said Month of* November, *at* St. Jago *de la Vega aforesaid.*

And of several Others, who were also condemn'd for PIRACY.

ALSO,

A True Copy of the Act of Parliament made for the more effectual suppression of Piracy.

Jamaica : Printed by *Robert Baldwin,* in the Year 1721.

PIRATES

JOSHUA B. FEDER

SMITHMARK

A FRIEDMAN GROUP BOOK

Copyright © 1992, 1996 by Michael Friedman Publishing Group, Inc.

This edition published in 1996 by SMITHMARK Publishers,
a division of U.S. Media Holdings, Inc.,16 East 32nd Street,
New York, New York 10016.

SMITHMARK books are available for bulk purchase for sales
promotion and premium use. For details write or call the manager
of special sales, SMITHMARK Publishers, 16 East 32nd Street,
New York, New York; (212) 532-6600.

ISBN 0-7651-9437-6

PIRATES
was prepared and produced by
Michael Friedman Publishing Group, Inc.
15 West 26th Street
New York, New York 10010

Editor: Dana Rosen
Art Director/ Designer: Devorah Levinrad
Photography Editor: Daniella Jo Nilva

Color Separations by Bright Arts Graphics (S) Pte Ltd
Printed in China by Leefung-Asco Printers Ltd.

DEDICATION

To my grandmother and her sister, Stella and Sabina, my first history teachers. I grew up on your stories and learned to appreciate history and understand how our lives are bound with the past.

ACKNOWLEDGMENTS

I would like to thank the staff of the New York Public Library for their patient assistance during my long hours of research. Special thanks to the staff of the rare maps division.

CONTENTS

INTRODUCTION: MYTH OR REALITY?

THROUGHOUT HISTORY HUMANKIND'S IMAGINATION has been captivated by the desperadoes of the high seas—pirates. Today, the commonly held vision of pirates is an extremely romanticized one. Many imagine a fearless swashbuckler, with one eye covered by an ominous black patch, firing a pistol from one hand and flashing a sword in the other while leaping about a ship with astounding acrobatic ability, easily defeating his foes. All the while his bandanna stays perfectly atop his head and a grin never leaves his face. After capturing mountains of glittering treasure, our brave pirate celebrates even harder than he fought: drinking inhuman amounts of rum, singing and dancing with reckless abandon, and of course, frolicking with women of dubious reputation. The "jolly pirate" is almost envied today because of his adventurous and free lifestyle. This popularly held vision of pirate life is constantly reinforced by motion pictures (Errol Flynn's films are a prime example) and in such popular amusement-park rides as Walt Disney's Pirates of the Caribbean.

Perhaps it is easy to appreciate pirates' attractive qualities today, now that they are long dead. Contemporaries of pirates, however, had no such luxury. For most of the last five thousand years—and piracy has been around for at least that long—the commonly held vision of a pirate was that of a ruthless thief and sometimes a sadistic murderer. Stories of unimaginable torture filled peoples' imaginations. One particularly notorious buccaneer of the seventeenth century earned the nickname "The Exterminator." With diabolic pleasure he would slice open a victim's belly, then pull out one end of the poor soul's entrails and nail it to a post. As if this were not enough, The Exterminator then pressed burning wood to his victim's bare bottom and watched as he contorted in a "ghastly dance of death to the limits of his insides, or his endurance." Even though every pirate was not as malicious as The Exterminator—indeed some pirates prided themselves on how well they treated their prisoners—rumors of such atrocities struck fear into any sane person who sailed the seas.

Various elements of popular culture, such as the pirate films featuring Errol Flynn, have greatly romanticized pirate life and personalities.

The buccaneers, a group of French and English runaway slaves, criminals, and deserters united by their hatred of anything Spanish, took to the seas in the mid-seventeenth century, ushering in an era of rampant piracy in the Caribbean.

Contrary to popular myths, pirates tried to avoid bloodshed whenever possible.

Authorities, although aware of the occasional torturing and murdering sprees, were more concerned with the chilling fact that rampant piracy virtually shut down important trade routes, causing famine and death in towns and cities. Under maritime law, pirates were considered *hostis humani generis*, "a common enemy" to all humankind, a fitting epithet since they belonged to no nation and preyed on any ship that had the bad luck to come into their grasp. To deter the culprits, authorities went to great lengths to capture

Pirates usually struck unsuspecting ships between two and six o'clock in the morning, using the cover of darkness and surprise as their weapons.

and brutally punish pirates. The punishment for "robbery on the high seas" was almost invariably public execution—if the pirate was lucky, this meant a quick hanging. Unlucky pirates captured by particularly vindictive authorities had the misfortune of being slowly roasted alive over burning hot coals. Pirates, almost the world over, were among the most detested criminals.

Quite possibly, the reason that many people today see piracy as such a romantic profession is that they really don't

After capturing a prize, pirates celebrated with drunken abandon.

know many of the basic facts regarding piracy. The current popular images of pirates—in motion pictures, as the mascot for the baseball team the Pittsburgh Pirates, or in the multitude of hotels and restaurants that operate under the name of the pirate flag, the Jolly Roger—provide a grossly distorted portrayal of pirate life. In reality, the average pirate never starred in a motion picture, certainly never played baseball, and was not especially fond of honest business or known for his culinary prowess. A typical pirate, who was almost always a man (with a few notable exceptions that will be discussed later), was neither terribly romantic nor unusually violent—he was simply trying to make a living. However, the pirate profession was (and still is) a remarkable and incredibly fascinating livelihood, in many ways far more unusual than popular images would lead one to believe.

PARTE ORIENTALE DEL
MEDITERRANEO
Del
Padre Cosmografo Coronelli
In Venezia, con Privilegio dell'Ecc.mo Senato

Coste della Dalmatia

ROMONIA

MACEDONIA

Golfo di Venezia, olim Adriaticum Mare

Mare di Toscana, et Thyrrenum

ISOLA DI SICILIA

MARIONIO
ò
DI GRECIA

MAR DE TRIPOLI

Coste de Tripoli

BARBARIA

MARE DI SAPIENZA

Mare di Candia

MARE DI BARCA

BARCA, olim M

Golfo de Sidra

1

THE PIRATE BASICS

FOR AT LEAST THE LAST FIVE THOUSAND YEARS, piracy has played a significant, but largely ignored, role in some of the truly epic events in history. As one historian put it, "Piracy at its greatest moments becomes a major part of history itself." Certainly such events as the Trojan War, the rise and fall of the Roman Empire, and the spread of Islam have been well documented, but the contribution made by pirates to these earth-shaking events has been sadly overlooked. Sea robbers have contributed to the high drama and outrageous humor that make up history, and their stories deserve to be told.

Before entering the fascinating world of piracy, it is important to understand exactly what piracy entails, as well as the distinction between piracy and its kindred spirit, privateering, a maritime activity with which it is often confused. Pirates, who still prowl the seas today, operate completely outside the laws of civilized society, preying on any ship that comes in sight, regardless of nationality. Privateers, on the other hand, no longer exist: they sailed under their country's flag and were armed with a commission, which was issued by their government, authorizing limited piratical exploits against enemy ships. Although privateering and piracy looked exactly the same from the deck of a victimized ship, the law treated the two differently.

Piracy played an essential role in the rise of Greek civilization. The Greek god Dionysus is portrayed here punishing pirates.

PIRATES AND PRIVATEERS

The distinction between pirate and privateer is often a difficult one for the historian to make, especially considering the fact that the distinction was almost nonexistent until the seventeenth century. In the ancient world, what we would call privateering was actually so widely practiced that governments did not even bother issuing commissions; robbery on the high seas was common practice. Indeed, the distinction cannot really be applied to the ancient world—every ship that set sail engaged in some form of what we would call piracy.

Also, there is the matter of perspective: one country's privateer was another's pirate. Such legendary privateers as the red-bearded Barbarossa brothers, England's Sir Francis Drake (who had the backing of the queen of England), and the United States' John Paul Jones, although considered national heroes by their countrymen, were considered nothing other than scoundrels and pirates by their victims.

Sir Francis Drake, perhaps the most famous privateer in history, seizing Spanish treasure ships.

Piracy in Ancient Times

As old as sea travel itself, piracy is an ancient and worldwide phenomenon. From the Persian Gulf to the Sea of China, from the Mediterranean to the Atlantic, piracy has plagued maritime travel like a recurring disease. Piracy first reared its ugly head when the waters of the ancient world became highways for trade: enterprising and daring individuals saw an opportunity to lighten the loads of well-stocked merchant ships and then sell the booty for 100 percent profit. The insatiable thirst for wealth, an ever-present force in human affairs, spurred pirates to plunder any ship they could get their hands on.

What might surprise some is that pirates did not just attack seagoing vessels. They sometimes grew so bold as to raid villages and cities along the coastline—even the great city of Rome was sacked by Vandal pirates in A.D. 455.

Ever since the first report of piracy around 3000 B.C., pirates have marauded and sometimes totally controlled maritime trade routes, making a decent living in the process and causing more than a few honest businessmen sudden bankruptcy. The first documented account of pirate activity comes from ancient Sumeria, an early civilization nestled between the Tigris and Euphrates rivers, in present-day Iraq. The citizens of Sumeria, relying on these two great rivers to transport most of the food that kept them alive, were hit hard by the Guti pirates, a particularly barbarous lot of nomadic sea dogs. On the brink of disaster, the Sumerians struck back with piratical attacks of their own, defeating the Guti pirates at their own game.

Not long after the Sumerians defeated the Guti, the first written law against piracy was enacted by the Babylonians, an ancient civilization that followed the Sumerians. Even though the city of Babylon was two hundred miles (320km) from the Persian Gulf, piracy was such a problem in the waterways of Babylonia that a law was added to their famous Hammurabi codes. The Hammurabi codes, carved into a black rock that can now be seen in Paris at the Louvre, outlined the laws of the Babylonian society. Piracy was proscribed as a serious crime with a serious punishment— death. The only way a guilty pirate could avoid death was to pay a fine of thirty times the value of the stolen cargo. Despite its severity, the first law was by all accounts a mediocre deterrent, stopping very few from engaging in piracy.

In the following centuries, piracy became so difficult to control in the Mediterranean Sea that many civilizations, rather than fight a battle they could not win, simply adopted piracy as standard policy. In Greece, for example, piracy

Achilles, standing on the right, makes his departure for the Trojan War. Pirates were considered heroes in ancient Greece.

played an absolutely essential role in the rise of the Mycenaean civilization during the fourteenth century B.C.; not only did the Mycenaeans forge their civilization during a great struggle to defeat crazed pirates from nearby islands, but the Mycenaeans themselves adopted piratical tactics in their conquest of the eastern Mediterranean. With incredible savagery, the Mycenaean warriors made a living out of sacking and pillaging ships and cities. For the first, but not last time in history, a civilization emerged based on piracy.

The Mycenaeans carried their piracy all the way to Asia Minor, where one of the most memorable sieges of all time took place—the Trojan War—which the epic poet Homer described with all its gruesome detail. Homer constantly refers to Achilles, Agamemnon, and Odysseus, the heroic paragons of Mycenaean manliness, as pirates; such terms as "sackers of cities" and "raiders" were used as terms of honor and respect. A man's reputation, according to Mycenaean culture, was directly proportional to his ability to kill men and take prizes. Piracy, on land and sea, was a way of life, fully sanctioned by the leaders and society of Mycenae.

Although the Mycenaeans were renowned for their ability to fight with equal prowess on land and sea, they were unable to withstand the flood of Indo-European invaders that crashed through Greece and Asia Minor after 1200 B.C. The Dorian invaders brought death and destruction, forcing many of the Mycenaeans, as well as the Etruscans of Asia Minor, to take to the sea to avoid extinction.

Once at sea, these homeless peoples headed for Egypt to begin a new life. However, they did not receive a warm welcome in Egyptian waters, where they were considered pirates. Ramses II and Ramses III, the pharaohs who enslaved the Jews, saw the "sea people" as a dangerous threat to Egypt and so launched an all-out campaign to drive them away. The Egyptians, well provisioned and superior in numbers, slaughtered many of the pirates, while the rest sped north.

Pirates and the Roman Empire

Ironically, the Egyptian campaign indirectly caused the formation of perhaps the greatest empire of all time: the Roman Empire. As the Egyptians forced the pirates north during the eleventh century B.C., many of the Etruscan sea rovers settled on the Italian peninsula; over the next several hundred years the Roman Empire slowly emerged.

As the Roman Empire collapsed, even the great city of Rome was vulnerable to pirate attacks. This tragic scene portrays Rome after the Vandals sacked the city.

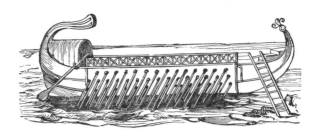

By the third century B.C., Roman power was impressive, but the Carthaginians of North Africa were the more dominant force. However, in 264 B.C., the Romans and the Carthaginians came to blows over a band of renegade pirates. The feud began when a group of fresh pirate converts, previously part of the king of Syracuse's mercenary squad, gained control of the narrow straits separating Sicily and Italy. The king of Syracuse, furious with his former soldiers, called upon the Carthaginians to help crush the pirates. Faced with swift and certain destruction, the pirates turned to the Romans for protection. Rome and Carthage moved inextricably toward a long and bloody confrontation. By the end of 264 B.C., war had broken out, and the Punic Wars, as they came to be known, would not end until 146 B.C. (During the second phase of the wars, Hannibal attempted his famous crossing of the Alps on elephants.) Piracy was the spark that ignited this tremendous conflict.

At the end of the Punic Wars, Rome emerged victorious and Carthage was destroyed. As with the Mycenaeans before, piracy had again played an essential role in the rise of a great empire. But unlike the Mycenaeans, the Romans did not turn to piracy themselves, instead opting for trade as the lifeblood of the incipient empire. However, the beginning of Rome's great empire did not mean the end of piracy.

Ironically, the seventy years following the end of the Punic Wars were a veritable golden age of piracy. Since Rome stubbornly stood by its land troops and stoutly refused to create a substantial navy to police the Mediterranean, pirates thrived as they attacked Roman trading ships with impunity. Kidnapping for ransom was also part and parcel of Mediterranean piracy, as illustrated by the capture of Julius Caesar. Rome, new to the responsibilities of being a great power, was suffering great losses at the hands of the pirates.

In the year 67 B.C., the Roman Senate, hounded by businessmen smarting from the sting of piracy, finally launched an incredibly coordinated and effective pirate-hunting campaign designed to eradicate all piracy from the Mediterranean. Led by the great general Pompey, two hundred warships and seventy smaller craft systematically swept the Mediterranean coasts, wiping out all of the land bases from which the pirates launched their attacks. Without land bases, the pirates were unable to resupply and mount any resistance to Pompey's forces; the pirates were sitting ducks on the Mediterranean pond. Pompey simply pounded the weakened pirates and, although the Cilician pirates put up a valiant fight, cleared the Mediterranean within a decade. For the first time in Mediterranean history, maritime travel was safe from piracy.

THE CAPTURE OF JULIUS CAESAR

Throughout the ages many famous people have had harrowing encounters with greedy pirates. Perhaps the most famous example is a young Roman who became the legendary emperor of Rome: Julius Caesar. Before his reign as emperor, Caesar set sail for Rhodes, where he intended to polish up his oratory skills under the great master Appolonius Molon. Caesar's ship was attacked by pirates near present-day Turkey, and all aboard were taken prisoner. As was the common custom, the pirates demanded a ransom for Caesar's safe return to his family. But when Caesar learned that the pirates were asking a mere twenty talents for his life, he indignantly told them he was worth at least fifty!

The pirates happily agreed to the immodest Roman's suggestion and had to wait only thirty-eight days to receive the ransom. During that time, the pirates treated the friendly and energetic Caesar graciously, even though they vehemently criticized the poetry that he composed while on board. The aspiring poet, in turn, behaved with civility but constantly berated the barbarians for not fully appreciating his poetic ability. Caesar vowed that his captors would be crucified for capturing the great Julius Caesar—perhaps because of their vicious condemnation of his poetry. But when the ransom finally arrived and Caesar was released, the pirates never thought they would see the self-important Roman again.

Caesar, however, fully intended to carry out his vow. After being released, the spurned poet went to the nearest port and raised a fleet. With little delay, Caesar captured the pirates and summarily crucified all of them, forever silencing his worst critics.

With control of virtually the entire Mediterranean coast, the Romans lived for centuries in relative peace. However, for myriad reasons, the empire began to fall apart in the third century A.D. Some historians claim that the infusion of Gothic barbarians from the north diluted the Roman Empire's leadership, while others suggest that a renewal of rampant piracy was responsible for the disintegration of Rome's control of the coasts. The truth probably lies somewhere in the middle: as the Goths mingled with the Romans, leadership faltered and control of the coasts began to slip away. Pirates, long inactive, struck hard at the chink in the great empire's armor, in turn weakening its leadership.

Whatever the explanation for the collapse of Rome's power, the size and power of the pirate fleets steadily grew. The Goths swarmed down from the Black Sea in A.D. 267, wreaking havoc in the eastern portion of the Mediterranean. In the west, King Gaiseric of the Vandals grew so powerful that his pirate fleet sacked Rome in A.D. 455; within forty years the Vandals had seized North Africa, taking a healthy chunk out of the Roman Empire. The sack of Rome and the loss of North Africa signified the nadir of Rome's power; piracy, which had been so important in the origin of the Roman Empire, was also partially responsible for its fall.

A New Breed of Pirates

Even though the Vandals now controlled the western waters of the Mediterranean, luxury goods still flowed from east to west, from Arabia and the Orient to the western regions of the European continent. Wonderfully exotic spices and glorious silks still made their way to European consumers, but only at substantial prices. The Vandals, impressive as they were, could not completely shut down trade by piracy.

Everything changed, however, when Islam spread like wildfire throughout the Arab world and North Africa. Before the seventh century A.D., the divisive tribal units of the Arabian peninsula were unable to mount any organized piratical campaign in the Mediterranean because they were too busy fighting each other. However, the religion of Islam, founded by Mohammad in the seventh century, welded the tribes into fierce fighting units, lessened the tribal infighting, and channeled hostilities toward the Europeans, otherwise known as the "infidels."

After the death of Mohammad, the Moslems consolidated their land and sea forces and rapidly expanded into Asia Minor and Northern Africa, which served as an ideal launching pad

Christopher Columbus explains his plans to circumvent Moslem-dominated Mediterranean trade routes by finding a western route to India. Ferdinand and Isabella, the king and queen of Spain, listen patiently.

for piratical activities in the Mediterranean. By A.D. 711, the reach of the growing Moslem empire had touched southern Spain, where the Moors remained until 1492. United by Islam, the Moslem leaders were ruthlessly efficient in their domination of the Mediterranean and their vast land empire, which covered most of the area separating Europe from the Orient. Due to the surge in Moslem power, Europeans were all but cut off from the luxury goods they craved so much.

Although Moslems did trade with the Europeans, piracy was the more common practice, with each side plundering the goods of the other. Moslem piracy, however, was unique because it was so closely associated with the religious doctrines of Islam. Islam, which means submission to Allah, actually gives divine sanction to piratical activities. Mohammad, himself a well-practiced highway robber, claimed that a

The morning of October 12, 1492, aboard the *Santa Maria*. Columbus, believing he had reached India, called the natives "Indians."

holy war, or *jihad*, against all infidels, whether Jew or Christian, entitled Moslems to use any means necessary to expel the infidels from Arab territory. Consequently, attacking non-Moslem prizes was actually a religious service, and success was considered a sign of divine blessing. In an odd way, the Moslems engaged in religious privateering, not piracy, and they sailed with a commission from the highest authority of all—Allah.

European Christians, however, did not recognize the word of Allah and wasted little time in challenging the Moslems' control of the trade routes to the Orient. By the eighth century, Moslems and Christians were engaged in a religious war on the Mediterranean, with the Italian cities leading the attack. As the Moslems and Christians, both employing piratical tactics, jockeyed for power on the Mediterranean during the fifteenth century, cities like Genoa and Venice grew rich from trade and piracy. Nevertheless, despite the growing wealth of the small merchant class, the Moslem grip on Eastern luxury goods was a sore spot for many Europeans.

One man, born in Genoa in 1451, was so dazzled by the wealth of the Orient that he could not stop imagining what staggering profits could be made if only a new route to the Orient could be found—a westward route that would circumvent the Moslem world and the dangers of the Mediterranean. He relentlessly tried to find financial backing for a daring voyage into the Atlantic, until he finally attained the support of the Spanish king and queen, Ferdinand and Isabella. Christopher Columbus was on his way to discovering the New World, and thereby shifting the center of trade from the Mediterranean to the Atlantic.

Noua Zemla · gelatur · Tabin prom · Polus Magnet

MARE TABIN

Petzorke morie

Alba · Margaster · Signium Dauidis nautæ · Saniam · Mocka pr.

Oceanus Hyperboreus

Zemla · Colgoyeue · Vagatz · Oby flu. · Tazata · Naiman

Mongul · Catacora · Vng · Belgian deser tum

Calami · Welikiperm · Gruftina

Pinego · Meshed · Citrachaw · Kasakhi

TARTARIA

EVROPA · Russia · Littauia · Moscouia · Cracaw

Bergen · Fane · Scotia · Anglia

Constanc.

S · I · A

Sam archand · Cotam · Prim · Mare Cin · Insulæ

Zechem · Caitachi

India Ori- ntalis · Iapan

Babylonia · Turbec · Chefmur

Cerzeli · Tunis · A interior · Aminon · Sagdech · Arabia

Lybia in terior · AFRI- · Aegyptus · Sinus Arabicus · Nubia

Lequio minor · Lequio

C · Mina · Agysym · Sabam · Nilus flu.

Ind. flu. · Caraparum · Decan · Calecut · Orixa · Golfo Bengala

Baruffe inf · Haina · Palohan · Burne · Sabuc · Cailon · Mindam

Mare rubrum · Zeilam insul · Data · Malaco · Moluccæ · Celebe

Verga · Iuftino · Nobon Insul · Manicongo · Abi ssini · Leuma

Magadaxo · Braua · Melinde · Zanzibar · Quiloa · Monzambique · Manope · Macace

MARE DI INDIA

Sunda · Iaua maior · Fideida · Cambaba · Bacular · Timortidor · Pecan

Beif · Oceanus æthiopicus

Insulay S. Lau rentij

Beach prouincia aurifera · Lucach regnum · Maletur regnum Sarci aromatibus · Iaua minor producit varia aromata Europeis nunquam vi

C. Negro · C. de tor rientes · C. Salido

Tristan de Acunna · Cayneca · Cor tada · Punta de S. Maria · Punca primera · C. de las Va cas · C. bonę Spei · Goncalo Aluares · Los Romeros

Vastissimas hic esse regiones ex
Pauli Veneti et Ludouici Varto
vi scripto...

Previous pages: A rare map of the world as seen in 1608. Above: This detail from a map of the Americas illustrates the abundance of gold and silver in the New World.

Pirates of the New World

In 1492, Columbus discovered the New World, which included the beautifully blue waters and splendid islands of the Caribbean. Columbus' patrons, Ferdinand and Isabella, unaware that the Caribbean would eventually become the stomping ground for some of the most legendary pirates of all time, claimed the entire hemisphere for Spain. For a while, nobody challenged Spain's claim. But after the Portuguese explorer Pedro Alvarez Cabral landed on the Brazilian coast of South America, Portugal demanded that Spain share the vast New World. Spain refused, but the Pope interceded in 1493, ordering the two Catholic countries to share the Western Hemisphere. Smarting from the papal order, Spain responded by announcing to Europe that only Spanish ships and settlements would be allowed in the Spanish half of the New World.

As the Spanish galleons brought mounds of gold and silver back to Europe during the early 1500s, along with tall tales of lush land, exotic peoples, and untold wealth, Spain's settlement policy became increasingly difficult to enforce. Hungry, bold adventurers from all over Europe, especially non-Catholics who did not recognize the pope's authority, ignored the Spanish ban on settlement and set sail for better lives in the New World.

After the defeat of the Spanish Armada by England in 1588, the pace of settlement increased, causing serious problems for Spain. Many of the new settlers had anything but honest intentions. In the early 1600s, a mangy group of runaway slaves, criminals, and deserters, most of whom were French, began roaming the savannas of northwestern Hispaniola, an island in the greater Antilles that is today divided between Haiti and the Dominican Republic. The unwelcome French settlers were originally ignored by the Spanish since these buccaneers—as they were called—did not bother anyone except the wild cattle and pigs that they hunted. Wearing odd peaked hats and clothes that were black and stiff from the blood of slaughtered animals, the buccaneers roamed in groups of two or three, butchering cattle and then curing the meat on *boucans,* the drying racks from which the buccaneers derived their name. In their spare time, buccaneers and their *matelots,* or partners, were known to become rather intoxicated, but so long as their numbers remained small, they were of little consequence to Spain. However, as events unfolded, these land-bound, carnivorous buccaneers were transformed into the sea-going buccaneers that terrorized Spanish shipping during the 1600s.

In the early 1600s, buccaneers eked out a meager living off wild cattle and pigs. But as time went on, they began trading with ships of all nations that were headed back to Europe, exchanging their delicious cured meat for ammunition and provisions. Quite often, sea-weary crewmen deserted ship and joined the French buccaneers, thereby diversifying and swelling their numbers, as well as attracting the attention of the Spanish. Facing an obvious violation of their settlement restrictions, the Spanish began hunting down the scattered clans of buccaneers; in danger of annihilation, most of the buccaneers fled to cattle-infested Tortuga, a small island shaped like the back of a sea turtle, just off the northwest coast of Hispaniola. The Spanish, at least for the moment, were satisfied that the problem was solved in Hispaniola.

Although the buccaneers were initially accepted by the Spanish settlers on Tortuga, they soon alienated their hosts when the island was turned into a giant curing house and a rowdy drinking hole. Once again, Spanish fleets were called upon to crush the buccaneer nuisance. In one day, the Spanish landed on Tortuga and all the buccaneers were routed; those lucky enough to escape headed back to Hispaniola, while many others were murdered. The Spanish, flushed with victory, pursued the buccaneers back to Hispaniola, where they continued to hunt them down.

The remaining buccaneers, a very resilient and crafty bunch, began organizing their resistance, grouping together and fighting the Spanish to a standstill. To break the stalemate, the Spanish began slaughtering the cattle upon which the buccaneers relied for survival. Outraged at the despicable Spanish ploy, the buccaneers, more united and powerful than ever before, surprised the Spanish by boldly sailing back to Tortuga *en masse*, sacking the island, and turning it into a well-fortified buccaneer sanctuary in 1630.

Despite repeated attacks, the Spaniards could not defeat the entrenched buccaneers. With a burning hatred for anything Spanish, the buccaneers recruited new members, with

Henry Morgan, a seventeenth-century English buccaneer, recruits new members for his attacks on Spanish galleons.

Cartographers of the seventeenth century illustrated their maps with battle scenes. This detail comes from an early seventeenth-century map of New Spain (today Mexico).

a strict ban on Spaniards. For the next ten years, they continued their buccaneering ways on Tortuga, slaughtering cattle and selling the meat to passing ships. Unfortunately for the Spanish, the cattle-butchering buccaneers soon gave way to the Spanish-butchering "Brothers of the Coast," buccaneers who took to the sea to get rich and to repay the Spanish for past injustices.

The boiling caldron of hatred that was Tortuga spilled into the Caribbean in 1640. Pierre Le Grand, the man credited with the first act of buccaneering—as it became known—set off from Tortuga with twenty-eight desperate men and a daring plan. Heading for the Windward Channel, an area bustling with Spanish galleons, Le Grand waited for a prize worth the risk he was planning to take.

With provisions running dangerously low, Le Grand finally spotted a fat galleon that had drifted from its fleet. Despite being outmanned by three to one and totally out-

A buccaneer poses with his unique rifle while smoking a pipe. Buccaneers were renowned for their marksmanship and practiced by tossing a doubloon, an old gold Spanish coin, in the air and shooting a hole through the middle.

gunned, Le Grand intended to board the galleon and sail away with the tremendous prize. Sure that his crew would not share his conviction, Le Grand gave them extra incentive when he had the ship's doctor bore holes in the hull of their own ship; there would be no turning back, victory or death were the only options.

Alexander Exquemelin, a French doctor who sailed with the buccaneers and later wrote a book about his adventures, described Le Grand's bold attack as follows: "It was in the dusk of the evening, or soon after, when this great action was performed." Armed with pistols and swords they swiftly "climbed up the sides of the ship, and ran altogether into the great cabin, where they found the captain, with several of his companions, playing at cards. Here they set a pistol to his breast, commanding him to deliver up the ship unto their obedience. The Spaniards, seeing the pirates aboard their ship, without scarce seeing them at sea, cried out, 'Jesus bless us! Are these devils, or what are they?'"

Exquemelin continues: "In the meanwhile, some of them took possession of the gun room, and seized the arms and military affairs they found there, killing as many of the ship as made any opposition. By which means the Spaniards were compelled to surrender." Unbelievably, Le Grand had succeeded just as his leaking boat sank into the sea.

News of Le Grand's smashing success spread quickly, prompting a torrent of piratical activity from fellow buccaneers. In no time at all the number of pirates increased so quickly that there were over twenty ships anchored at the island of Tortuga. These buccaneers called themselves Brothers of the Coast, a fraternity bonded together by hatred of the Spanish and love of the sea.

The Brothers of the Coast were peculiarly principled for members of such a low-down profession. Technically, the buccaneers were not really pirates; instead of attacking all ships regardless of nationality, the buccaneers attacked only Spanish ships, making a point of torturing their Spanish prisoners. But by 1697, the Spanish presence in the New World was greatly reduced, removing the target of the buccaneers' venom. Buccaneering flashed through the Caribbean with intensity for less than one hundred years, and then faded away as the Spanish presence dwindled.

However, the great success of the Brothers of the Coast quickly inspired a less-principled lot of sea rovers to go a-pirating, men who had no intention of limiting their attacks to Spanish ships. During the eighteenth and nineteenth centuries, hordes of avaricious men, as well as a few women, from

Howard Pyle, a nineteenth-century illustrator, was famous for his many pirate scenes. In this illustration, buccaneers taunt the captain of a seized galleon.

around the world descended on maritime trade routes. Particularly in the West Indies, Madagascar, and the Malabar Coast of India, a modern, well-organized breed of piracy emerged after the wane of the buccaneers. Many of the great myths and legends that are with us today arose from the exploits of these flamboyant, ruthless pirates. These sea robbers, discussed in detail in the following chapters, were the final product of the evolution of piracy; they represent the pinnacle of pirate laws, battle tactics, and customs.

Laws, Battle Tactics, and Customs

What kind of man became a pirate, and why did he opt for a career in piracy? Pere Labat, years after casting his lot with the buccaneers, suggested that "The pirates are, as a rule, filibusters who have grown so accustomed to this free life in times of war, when they generally hold commissions, that they cannot make up their minds to return to work when peace is made, and therefore continue their roving." Labat is referring to the common practice of privateering (sometimes called filibustering), a legalized breed of piracy, which produced many famous pirates.

Privateering was a common practice from ancient Greece until the War of 1812. During wartime, governments issued special commissions, commonly known as Letters of Marque in eighteenth-century Europe, which gave privately owned ships the authority to attack and plunder enemy shipping. When the wars ended, so did the privateering licenses, throwing these seamen out of a job. Rather than return to dry land, a frightful prospect for a man of the sea, and almost certain

FAMOUS BUCCANEERS

The Brothers of the Coast were not interested in fame or glory: they merely wanted to live life to the fullest and bring as much pain and suffering to the Spanish as possible. Thus, even though as many as five thousand buccaneers sailed the Caribbean, only a few of the names have come down to us, these thanks to the documentation of Alexander Exquemelin.

Bartolomeo the Portuguese, a native Portuguese who came to the New World as a teenager, was a buccaneer who had an unusual career. Constantly being captured by the Spanish, Bartolomeo had a knack for escaping the most precarious situations, even though he couldn't swim. On one occasion Bartolomeo was captured after his ship ran aground. His captor, intending to hang him the next day and knowing that he could not swim, locked Bartolomeo on board a ship. In the middle of the night, Bartolomeo killed the guard with a knife and then floated ashore, holding himself above water with a pair of empty wine jugs. Not long after, he returned to his floating prison and stole the ship right out from under the nose of his previous captor.

Another buccaneer known as L'Olonnois was perhaps the most sadistic buccaneer of all. L'Olonnois took pleasure in murdering Spanish prisoners and inventing bizarre rituals to frighten the prisoners before putting them out of their misery. Once he lined up eighty-seven prisoners in a row and then personally walked down the line, stopping only long enough to lop off each prisoner's head with his sword.

On another occasion, L'Olonnois, losing his temper with a group of Spanish prisoners, cut out the heart of one man and fed it to another—an act surely consistent with his nickname, "The Cruel."

Fittingly, L'Olonnois's life ended when he was taken prisoner by Indians after his ship broke up in a storm. As Exquemelin put it, the Indians "tore him to pieces alive, throwing his body limb by limb into the fire and his ashes into the air; to the intent no trace nor memory might remain of such an inhuman creature."

Pirates collecting their share of a prize. Any attempt to cheat a fellow pirate was punishable by death.

unemployment, many privateers instead continued with what they knew best, without a license. Once outside the law, pirates answered to no nation, attacking all ships with equal vigor. Oddly enough, privateers never really changed their life-style or battle tactics; it was the outside world that changed around them and now considered them criminals.

Ex-privateers alone did not account for the continual flow of fresh pirate recruits. A major source of new blood flowed from the decks of the merchant and naval ships that were captured by pirates. Often, life on these ships was dismal; men drearily looked forward to pitiful wages (if any at all), terrible food, and frequent beatings from despotic captains. Some captains treated their crews so badly that deaths were not uncommon. One captain was reported to flog his men until they were "a gory mass of flesh" and force them to swallow live cockroaches. Other captains frequently punished by "keel-hauling" the offender—dragging the man right under the shell-encrusted keel of the boat. It comes as no surprise that when these haggard and abused men saw a pirate ship on the horizon, they were not afraid, had little intention of putting up a fight, and probably saw an opportunity for a new and better life-style. These men were rarely forced to turn pirate, but they very often decided that life as one would be better.

While the converts from merchant and naval ships continually filled the ranks of pirates, a few individuals turned to piracy for other, more peculiar reasons. One unusual convert was Major Stede Bonnet, a respected gentryman from Barbados, who bought and fitted out a sloop from his own purse, a costly and unprecedented purchase, turning to piracy to get away from a nagging wife! Bartholomew Roberts, perhaps the orous, romantic adventure—as today's popular images would suggest—but rather a plain and simple business system.

Just like any other business, piracy, especially between the seventeenth and nineteenth centuries, followed certain well-defined rules. Since the tantalizing prospect of getting rich quickly attracted some rather unsavory characters, these pirate codes were necessary to keep fellow conspirators from cutting each other's throats to get more money. The laws that governed a particular pirate ship were outlined in the Captain's Articles, a type of contract that was drawn up and signed by all hands before a pirate ship set sail. The following contract, "The Articles of Captain Phillips" (1723), is a good example of the basic laws that governed pirate life:

1. Every man shall obey civil command; the captain shall have one full share and a half in all prizes; the master, carpenter, boatswain, and gunner shall have one share and a quarter.

2. If any man shall offer to run away, or to keep any secret from the company, he shall be marooned, with one bottle of powder, one bottle of water, one small arm [pistol] and shot.

3. If any man shall steal any thing in the company, or game to the value of a piece of eight, he shall be marooned or shot.

4. If at any time we should meet another marooner [pirate] that man that shall sign his articles without the consent of our company shall suffer such punishment as the captain and company shall think fit.

5. That man that shall strike another whilst these articles are in force shall receive Moses's Law (that is, forty stripes lacking one) on the bare back.

6. That man that shall snap his arms, or smoke tobacco in the hold without a cap to his pipe, or carry a candle lighted without a lanthorn, shall suffer the same punishment as in the former article.

7. That man that shall not keep his arms clean, fit for an engagement, or neglect his business, shall be cut off from his share, and suffer such other punishment as the captain and the carpenter shall think fit.

8. If any man shall lose a joint in time of an engagement, he shall have four hundred pieces of eight; if a limb, eight hundred.

9. If at any time we meet with a prudent woman, that man that offers to meddle with her, without her consent, shall suffer present death.

Major Stede Bonnet dangling from the gallows in 1718. Friends placed flowers in his shackled hands.

most successful pirate of all time, was taken prisoner by pirates and, being an honest seaman, was originally disinclined to join his captors. Making the best of a situation from which he could not escape, however, he later became captain of the ship because, as he was reported to say, "since I have dipped my hands in muddy water, and must be a pyrate, it is better being a commander than a common man."

For whatever reason a man became a pirate, he chose a way of life remarkably similar throughout time and throughout the world. Pirates, in general, have adhered to the same laws, implemented the same battle tactics, and followed the same customs, regardless of time and place. What is most striking about worldwide piracy is that it was rarely considered a glam-

By voluntarily signing this contract, each crewmember was going "on the account," as the eighteenth-century pirates called it. Once on the account, the seafarer, now considered a pirate, accepted the virtually universal law of all pirates— what the British called "No Prey, No Pay." There was no guaranteed salary, no weekly wage for pirates; payday came when a ship was captured. All seized booty went into a common pool and was then distributed according to a share system, with each pirate earning a specified number of shares that were commensurate with his responsibilities. For all intents and purposes, the pirate ship was a floating stock company, which only payed dividends after a ship was captured.

During battle, this pirate captain had total authority over his crew. But no captain had dictatorial powers during peacetime, when decisions were arrived at democratically.

The business structure of piracy was almost identical throughout the world. Mrs. Ching, the most successful female pirate ever, based her Chinese pirate fleet on the same kind of share system as Captain Phillips, with an Oriental twist. Article two of Mrs. Ching's articles read, "Not the least thing shall be taken privately from stolen and plundered goods. All shall be registered, and the pirate receive for himself of ten parts, only two." Mrs. Ching, a product of Oriental piracy, which many consider far more authoritarian and hierarchical than Western piracy, took a much higher percentage of the loot for herself: 80 percent, to be exact.

The share system, although efficient, worked only so long as trust and order were maintained. Keeping order amongst such a motley crowd was difficult, even when the whole crew was sober (which wasn't very often), but absolutely essential to the smooth operation of a pirate venture. To keep the crew in line, punishable offenses included stealing from the company, desertion, cowardice, and fighting on board.

Stealing and desertion were particularly serious crimes because they directly undermined the share system that held the pirates' stock company together. The punishment, marooning, reflected the gravity of the crimes. Being marooned on a small island was perhaps the ultimate fear of the sea-loving pirates. The offender, sarcastically called "governor of an island," was given water and left to die an agonizingly slow death, with hunger whittling away the culprit's body. Pirates would sometimes leave the marooned man a small pistol to end his life if the pain became unbearable.

Although punishment was swift and deadly on board pirate vessels, there were no despotic captains who meted out unjustified floggings. Indeed, so many pirates had endured life under brutal merchant captains that they ensured freedom from such despotism on pirate ships. The captain was elected by the crew, usually for his fighting and leadership ability, but his tenure only lasted as long as his popularity; at any time the captain could be voted out of office. Also, much to the captain's chagrin, he had real authority only during battle, when the crew followed his every order. But once a battle or chase was over, the captain's authority was diminished and his crew rambunctiously disobeyed any order they pleased. The bottom line, as one contemporary put it, was that "They only permit him to be captain on condition that they may be captain over him." In most cases, pirate ships were a floating democracy, dangerously close to anarchy.

With articles signed and a captain elected, a pirate ship set off in search of prey. Once on the prowl, certain policies

Above: Now and then a pirate crew would kill a captain instead of voting him out of office. Below: Duels were a popular way of selecting candidates for a vacant captaincy. These duels were not fought to the death but only until one man had clearly overpowered the other.

were followed to ensure maximum profit with minimum risk. One article widely practiced and consistently observed by pirates in general, and especially by the pirates of the West Indies, was that good quarter shall be given to all who ask for it. This policy was not motivated by any kind of morality, but rather practicality. Pirates did not want to fight if it could be avoided. Consequently, an offer of good quarter, signaled by the black flag or Jolly Roger, was intended to persuade the frightened victims to lay down their weapons and offer no resistance. If there was no resistance, then the pirates promised not to harm prisoners, especially women.

However, if the cornered ship refused to acknowledge the Jolly Roger, then the pirates hoisted the red flag (preferably dipped in blood), which meant death for all aboard. Quite often, as the crew pondered the offer of good quarter, the idea of following an abusive merchant captain in the defense of a ship and cargo that belonged to some rich merchant seemed absurd. So, rather than see the red flag hoisted and face almost certain death, many a crew simply handed over the ship.

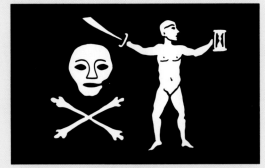

Captain Walter Kennedy

Captain Emanuel Wynne

Captain Jack Rackham

The pirate flag, known as the Jolly Roger, was designed to strike fear into potential victims. The Jolly Roger was an offer of good quarter and a warning of what might happen if the offer was refused. The skull and crossbones represented death, and the hourglass meant that the trapped crew needed to make a quick decision. If the crew did not surrender quickly, the pirates would raise a red flag, which meant the offer of good quarter had been withdrawn. Many successful pirate captains revised the pirate flag to their own specifications. Shown here are several customized versions of the Jolly Roger.

Captain Thomas Tew

Captain Edward England

Captain Henry Avery

Captain Bartholomew Roberts

Captain Bartholomew Roberts

Blackbeard

Captain Stede Bonnet

Captain Christopher Condent

WALKING THE PLANK

Pirates sometimes tortured their unfortunate prisoners in many imaginative and sadistic ways. The most well-known (yet rarely practiced) way to send a prisoner to his death was to force him to "walk the plank." The man often credited with inventing this fiendish death walk is Major Stede Bonnet, an eighteenth-century gentleman who apparently turned to piracy because, as Daniel Defoe explained, "the Major's mind had become unbalanced owing to the unbridled nagging of Mrs. Bonnet."

Although walking the plank was not as common as the punishment of simply throwing prisoners overboard, neither was practiced with much frequency until the eighteenth century. During the eighteenth and nineteenth centuries, many European nations abolished slavery and the slave trade. Until that time pirates had sold prisoners into slavery, making a tidy profit, and since slaves could not testify in a court of law, silencing witnesses to the pirates' crimes. With slavery outlawed, the pirates were forced to come up with new ways to keep their prisoners from talking to the authorities. Consequently, many pirates turned to murder as a way of keeping witnesses dead quiet.

Sometimes the pirates did meet resistance, or they chose not to offer quarter, preferring to use surprise as a weapon. When a pirate ship swung into battle, it was an ugly sight. As was often the case, the pirate ship was much smaller than its prey, so the crew relied on speed and cunning, not brute force, to capture a prize. A broadside cannon duel with a ship that usually outgunned the pirates' vessel by five to one—despite what motion pictures might suggest—would have been suicidal. Besides the horrible odds, smashing solid cannon balls through the hull of a prize would sink it, along with valuable cargo—the last thing greedy pirates wanted to do.

Thus, pirate ships always approached off the bow of the target, getting close enough so that the gunners could fire balls connected by chains into the masts of the ship. The chain shot buzzed through the air with incredible force, shredding any ropes, sails, or humans that were in its path.

A crew evacuates a burning merchantman. Attacking pirates tried to avoid setting fire to ships because the ship itself was a valuable prize.

Always careful to avoid the hull, the intent was to immobilize the ship, not destroy it.

As the pirates gained on the disabled ship, they fired canvas bags of "angrage," a devilish mix of nails, nuts, and bolts, which sprayed onto the enemy's decks. Now close enough to board the ship, the pirates relied on the cutlass and the pistol for hand-to-hand combat. Throwing grappling hooks over the rails of the disabled prey, the daring pirates scurried onto the deck, where they were masters with the blade. Usually, the battle was quick and bloody, with heavy losses for the pirates, but even heavier for their victims.

If the seized ship was a sturdier vessel than their own, the pirates would not hesitate to abandon their old ship or sail away with both to start a pirate fleet. After capturing a prize, pirates were eager to divide the treasure and celebrate. Quite often, the pirates would look for a secluded bay or cove, ideally rimmed with tall trees, and beach the ship for an onshore party. The respite also provided an opportunity to careen, or clean the hull of the ship, a task that was necessary every two or three months to maintain the ship's speed and maneuverability. Careening, which involved tilting the ship to one side and scraping the shell-encrusted hull clean, was extremely dangerous because the pirates were vulnerable to attack by other ships. However, they dealt with the anxious situation by celebrating with reckless abandon, forgetting the great risk they were taking. Indeed, many of the traditional pirate customs evolved as a way of dealing with the often boring, and sometimes dangerous, life on the high seas.

Careening was a time for carousing. Hard liquor was the drink of choice, some saying "good liquor to a sailor is preferable to clothing." Many pirates drank because they thought it was good for their health, while others simply enjoyed the camaradarie alcohol inspired. In a drunken stupor, pirates cavorted like wild dogs—singing, dancing, play-acting, and staging mock trials where the pirates pretended to be both judge and prisoner, a parody of a real-life situation they might find themselves confronting one day.

"The Pirate is truly fond of women and wine," said Charles Ellms in *The Pirate's Own Book* (1837). Although liquor was more abundant than women, pirates enjoyed both when they had the chance. Certainly the pirate is legendary for his fondness for women, but little is said about the sexual relations amongst the pirates themselves. Homosexuality was quite common and accepted. Indeed, on Captain Bartholomew Roberts' ships the following article was in effect: "No boy or woman allowed among us." The article was intended to prevent

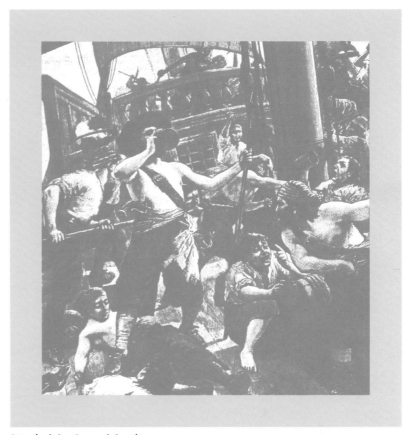

A typical drunken celebration.

a boy or woman from causing jealousy or fighting amongst the crew. Also, the pirates' active sex lives meant that venereal diseases were a serious problem.

After careening and carousing, the pirates, some questioning the pointlessness of their lives, set out to sea to hunt down another ship. Far from being a jolly profession, piracy was an oddly manic career, with swings of joy and depression, excitement and boredom. Pirate life was usually short, but it was filled with intense memories.

Despite the drawbacks, piracy always attracted new recruits, eager to live life to the fullest. However, by the mid-nineteenth century fewer and fewer pirates sailed the seas. With the introduction of the wireless radio, steam power, and steel ships, the policing of maritime trade routes was far more effective than ever before. The pirates, still bound to wooden sailboats, could not compete. But, as the following stories illustrate, piracy right before its demise was practiced with relish by tens of thousands of particularly unusual knaves, villains, gentlemen, and women around the globe.

2

WILLIAM KIDD

CAPTAIN WILLIAM KIDD IS PERHAPS THE MOST well-known sea dog of all time. His legendary piratical exploits between the years 1696 and 1700 earned him a larger-than-life reputation as a tyrannical captain, a mercilessly sadistic torturer, and a brutally efficient pirate. In addition, outrageous rumors of Kidd's vast buried treasures still spark the imagination of treasure hunters around the world. In the four years during which Kidd plagued the high seas, his name not only echoed through the dark, dingy taverns of England and its North American colonies but also bellowed through the great halls of the English Parliament. If pirates were measured by words alone, Captain Kidd would be the most outstanding pirate of all time.

But words alone do not make a great pirate. Ironically, Kidd's reputation far outweighs his actual deeds. As a pirate, he was a nominal success, a "third-rate pirate and a fourth-rate gentleman," when compared with other, lesser-known pirates of the time. But Kidd was uniquely unlike his fellow scoundrels: his great rise and fall were intimately tied to a tangled web of political intrigue that reached all the way to the king of England. When Kidd was finally arrested in Boston in 1700 and sent to London, his trial became a battlefield for the Whigs and the Tories, the political parties of England.

As a result, Captain Kidd's short and unimpressive career was transformed into a major public sensation.

William Kidd was an unusual candidate for piracy. Born in Greenock, Scotland, in 1645, Kidd was raised in relative affluence and received a solid, well-rounded education. As a young man, he was enchanted by the sea, so he joined the crew of a merchantman anchored in his hometown's harbor. Once on the rolling waves of the Atlantic, Kidd distinguished himself as an outstanding seaman and honest businessman, eventually earning command of his own merchant vessel.

Although successful as a merchant captain, the challenges of commanding a merchant vessel proved uninspiring to Kidd, who was in search of a better test of his abilities. Bored with his mundane merchant command, he seized an exciting opportunity to become an English privateer in search of French prey. He was a smashing success: he rose to the challenge and so successfully marauded French shipping that he was considered a hero in England and a ruthless scoundrel in France. Significantly, Kidd also became very well acquainted with the habits and hiding places of Atlantic pirates, knowledge that would be of great importance in his later career.

With a stellar record of national service, Kidd settled in New York City, where he married a wealthy woman and started a family. An established businessman and respected citizen, Kidd continued his patriotic ways: he often patrolled the New England waters and drove away enemy privateers or pirates. In 1691, he earned the undying gratitude of his neighbors when he gallantly confronted an enemy privateer and drove it far away from the New England coast. As a reward, his fellow New Yorkers voted to give the great Captain Kidd a cash bonus for his service.

Perhaps basking in the praise—and money—of his neighbors, Kidd kept up his protective service until his ship was stolen from right under his nose. While anchored off the island of Antigua in the West Indies, his crew mutinied, turned pirate, and then sailed away with his ship while Kidd was ashore. Apparently, the leader of the mutiny, a Madagascar man, had been able to persuade the rest of the crew that becoming pirates would make them rich men, an argument that proved irresistible for even the most loyal members of Kidd's crew. The success stories about Madagascar pirates like Captain Tew and Captain Maze finally convinced the crew to go on the account themselves.

The enraged Kidd, cursing his misfortune while stranded on Antigua, swore that he would never let another Madagascar man aboard his future ships.

The crew's sudden turn to piracy, although annoying to Kidd, was not an uncommon phenomenon at the time. Piracy was on the rise towards the beginning of the eighteenth century: not only were richly laden Spanish galleons and Portuguese merchantmen seductive targets for greedy seamen, but as a result of Parliament's passing of a series of Navigation Acts at the end of the seventeenth century, English ships were also coming under attack.

The reason that the Navigation Acts fueled the fire of piracy is quite simple. The acts forbade the American colonies from trading with other nations or producing any finished goods of their own—England was to be the sole buyer and distributor throughout their New World holdings. Consequently, English manufacturers charged exorbitant prices for their goods, enraging the handcuffed colonists. The colonists complained bitterly about the unfair prices, but even though their pleas fell on deaf ears in the mother country, another group heard the message loud and clear.

Pirates, always entrepreneurs, gambled that the disgruntled colonists would not mind if various sea rovers simply hijacked English ships and then sold the goods in the Ameri-

Above: Lord Bellomont. The man who enlisted William Kidd as captain of the *Adventure Galley*. Opposite page: The original coat of arms of the East India Company.

can colonies at reasonable prices. Swinging into action, some pirates traveled all the way to Madagascar to prey on the ships of the British East India Company, while other pirates, like Blackbeard, used North American bases to launch their Atlantic expeditions. The pirates had hit the jackpot; feeding the insatiable demand in the colonies kept them very busy and very wealthy.

The surge of piracy toward the end of the seventeenth century finally reached epidemic proportions, forcing the English government to take action. The East India Company, especially hard hit by the Madagascar pirates, used all of its lobbying power to pressure the politicians into curtailing piratical activity. Although Parliament sluggishly refused to take formal action, many individual members personally financed pirate-hunting expeditions. Although these financiers were interested in protecting their country's interests, many were not above taking a hefty portion of the booty captured from pirates. Thus, profit, not just patriotism, motivated many of the members of Parliament. But whatever their motives, the English were finally addressing the epidemic of piracy.

One particular group of Whig politicians worked especially hard to organize a profitable expedition. The only thing the politicians needed to make their pirate-hunting scheme work was a trustworthy captain. Captain Kidd, with his long history of public service and his hatred of Madagascar pirates, was the obvious candidate to head a vindictive pirate-catching campaign.

Lord Bellomont, a Whig and governor of New York, Massachusetts, and New Hampshire, contacted Captain Kidd, who happened to be in London at the time, with the offer to head the campaign. Bellomont, recently appointed by King William III, was ordered to use any means necessary to subdue the pirates, and his position depended on him choosing an honest captain. Kidd heartily accepted the offer, giddy with the prospect of avenging the loss of his ship.

The wealthy Whig backers of Kidd's campaign provided everything he needed. A fine, seaworthy ship, the *Adventure Galley*, was personally fitted out by Kidd, who made sure that the 284-ton (258t) ship was well armed and the crew honest—there was not one Madagascar man allowed on board. But even though Kidd was ready to set sail from England, he needed a commission to authorize his actions. Without the commission, Kidd would be no better than a pirate.

Bellomont and the other Whig backers were so influential that they procured a Royal Commission issued by King William III himself. The commission read:

William the Third, by the Grace of God, King of England, Scotland, France and Ireland, Defender of the Faith, &c. To our trusty and well beloved Captain William Kid, Commander of the ship the Adventure Galley, GREETING: Whereas we are informed, that Captain Thomas Tew, John Ireland, Captain Thomas Wake, and Captain William Maze, and other subjects, natives or inhabitants of New York, and elsewhere, in our plantations in America, have associated themselves, with divers others, wicked and ill disposed persons, and do, against the law of nations, commit many and great pyracies, robberies and depredations on the seas upon the parts of America, and in other parts, to the great hinderance and discouragement of trade and navigation, and to the great danger and hurt of our loving subjects, our allies, and all others.... Now KNOW YE, that we...do hereby give and grant the said William Kid...a commission as a private Man of War, bearing date the 11th Day of December 1695, with full power and authority to apprehend, seize, and take into your custody... all such pyrates, free Booters, and sea rovers.

In addition to this Royal Commission, Kidd was encouraged to attack the ships of France, a nation at war with England. Armed with thirty-four heavy guns and a Royal Commission, Kidd left in May of 1696.

But the pirate-hunting adventure got off to a poor start. Shortly after weighing anchor, the *Adventure Galley* was stopped by the *H.M.S. Duchess*, an English naval vessel, and the commander impressed, or forced, part of Kidd's crew into the British Navy. Smarting from the loss of honest seamen to the navy ship, Kidd limped toward New York, where he hoped to take on new hands.

The pickings in New York were slim: most of the experienced seamen that Kidd could find were hardened criminals. Consequently, Kidd was forced to enlist some rather unsavory characters, more than a few of whom were undoubtedly pirates themselves. By September of 1696, Kidd and his motley crew were ready to leave New York in search of pirates.

The great pirate enclave of Madagascar, an island off the southeast coast of Africa, was Kidd's first destination. The island was the base of Captain Tew and Captain Maze, two of his targets, who had been inflicting serious losses on the East India Company. However, as Kidd traveled east, he became increasingly aware that he might not have to wait until Madagascar to find pirates—his own crew was secretly talking about going on the account.

Kidd desperately tried to squelch the rising mutiny, but the crew's grumblings grew louder after a series of misfortunes hit the *Adventure Galley*: a vicious cholera epidemic killed many of the crew, the ship sprang several nasty leaks, and supplies reached dangerously low levels. Hobbling toward Madagascar with a mutinous crew, Kidd could only hope that his fortunes would turn once he reached Madagascar.

Captain Kidd's hopes were dashed when he arrived at Madagascar only to find that every pirate was out roving the sea in search of prey. Running low on supplies—and morale—Kidd headed his ship further east toward another pirate stomping-ground, the Malabar Coast of India. En route, the *Adventure Galley* sighted a number of fat Dutch and English ships, which Kidd hailed and let pass safely; an honest man, he was not about to attack innocent ships.

But Kidd's mutinous crew was enraged when he let such tantalizing prizes slip away. Many of them had had enough. Once the *Adventure Galley* anchored off the Malabar Coast, Kidd's crew dwindled as men mysteriously disappeared, slipping away to join the very pirates that Kidd was trying to catch. Despite his misfortunes, the honest Captain Kidd stubbornly refused to turn pirate, so he set off with his remaining crew to carry out his mission.

The remaining crew did not share Kidd's enthusiasm—or his honesty. One day, as the murmurs of mutiny were swelling to a roar, the gunner, William Moore, lost his temper and got into an heated argument with the captain. Moore shouted at Kidd, "You have brought us to ruin and we are desolate!" Flabbergasted at Moore's insubordination, Kidd picked up a heavy wood bucket and threw it at Moore's head, striking him squarely. Moore crumbled to the deck with a fractured skull and died the following day.

Deeply unnerved by Moore's open defiance and only slightly regretful about killing him, Kidd knew that he would be the next one to die unless he did something to placate his angry, frustrated, and hungry crew. The decision was made: Kidd swallowed his pride and went on the account.

After his fateful decision, Kidd went on a piratical rampage. Venting his frustration as a failed pirate-catcher, he proved a much better pirate. Cleverly, Kidd's first move was to bring down the British flag and hoist the French flag (all ships at the time carried numerous flags and documents so they could change identity as needed). Predictably, almost every captain he approached also hoisted the French flag. Once he saw the French colors, Kidd felt justified in attacking the ship since France was at war with England. However, this ploy was a very shaky cover for what most people called outright piracy.

News spread quickly, and England soon got wind of Kidd's turn to piracy. At first, the politicians, especially Kidd's Whig backers, tried to overlook his creative tactics because he was inflicting damage to French shipping. The situation changed, however, when Kidd began nabbing ships that were obviously not French, even if they did fly French colors. In February 1698, Kidd sealed his own fate when he captured his greatest prize of all, the *Quedagh Merchant*.

In Kidd's eyes, the *Quedagh* was a lawful prize because it was flying French colors. Conveniently overlooking the fact that the skipper was a friendly Englishman, the owner an Indian, and the cargo the property of Armenians, Kidd seized the five-hundred-ton (454t) ship along with the valuable cargo of silks, satins, gold, silver, and other luxury items. Kidd, knowing full well that the French flag and papers that the *Quedagh* had originally produced were forgeries, nonetheless took them to be genuine. This sleight of hand, at least in Kidd's mind, justified grabbing the *Quedagh*.

Pleased with his catch, Captain Kidd returned to Madagascar in the *Adventure Galley* with the *Quedagh* in tow. Upon reaching the island, Kidd transferred his crew from the waterlogged *Adventure Galley* to the more seaworthy *Quedagh*. From the decks of his new ship, Kidd watched as Captain Culliford's pirate ship glided to his side. No battle

ensued; Kidd made no attempt to capture the pirates he was supposed to bring to justice. Instead, Kidd brought Culliford on board and gave the man a drink, saying, "Before I would do you any harm, I would have my soul fry in hell." Later, when Kidd was on trial, he had a very difficult time explaining his friendliness with Culliford.

At the celebration on board the *Quedagh*, Kidd's crew was so impressed with Culliford that ninety-seven of them joined his ranks. But Kidd was not upset with the loss; he still had a

Captain Kidd claimed that he buried his treasure on Gardiner's Island. But pirate captains rarely had any substantial treasure to bury because the loot was distributed amongst the entire crew. Although many treasure hunters have searched for Kidd's treasure, it has never been found.

Lord Bellomont betrays William Kidd and puts him under arrest.

functioning crew and, of course, the wonderful *Quedagh*. At this point, Kidd decided it was time to return to New York City, where he could resume his place in society and be with his family. Looking forward to his homecoming, Kidd started the five-month journey from Madagascar to the West Indies.

While Kidd was rounding the tip of Africa, news of the *Quedagh*'s capture was having intense political repercussions in England and India. The Great Mogul of India, incensed that an English privateer had seized an Indian-owned ship, retaliated by throwing East India Company officials in jail. Smarting from the imprisonment of its eastern representatives, the East India Company pressured Parliament and the king to do something to appease the Great Mogul. The politicians, embarrassed that Kidd was sailing with a Royal Commission, responded by revoking the commission and proclaiming Kidd a pirate. The word was out to "pursue and seize the said Kidd and his accomplices."

At that time, the unsuspecting Kidd was nearing the island of Anguilla in the West Indies, where he was in for a big surprise. When his crew went ashore to get supplies, they came rushing back with the news that Kidd had been declared a pirate. Quickly unfurling his sails, Kidd headed to Antigua to figure out his plan of action. Hounded by ships out to catch him, he decided that his only hope was to explain his defense to Lord Bellomont, who would then rally the Whig backers who had originally financed the expedition.

But no sooner had Kidd come up with this plan than a man-of-war appeared on the horizon, forcing him to dash off to Hispaniola before he could get word to Bellomont. At Hispaniola, Kidd sold the *Quedagh* and purchased the *Antonio*, a smaller, less conspicuous sloop, which would allow Kidd to head toward New York unnoticed. Once again, Kidd was unable to send a letter to Bellomont before the man-of-war picked up his trail.

William Kidd in full garb on the deck of the *Adventure Galley.* Pirates believed that piercing the ears and wearing an earring improved vision. This idea was scoffed at for centuries, but acupuncture theory suggests that there is a point on the ear lobe that controls the eyes.

Traveling north to the Delaware Bay, Kidd put most of his crew ashore at Cape May. Although he was left with a skeleton crew and a respectable treasure, the disembarking crew had taken a major portion of the booty with them. Floating a little lighter in the water, Kidd finally sent his letter to Bellomont before speeding north—toward his doom.

Anxious to see his wife, Kidd proceeded to Gardiner's Island, just east of Long Island. Once anchored, he sent for his wife and several close friends to help plan his next move. Awaiting the tearful reunion, Kidd, sensing that his future was uncertain, used the time to bury his treasure (or so he later claimed). His wife's arrival did little to lift Kidd's spirits, for they could not decide what to do next.

Their luck seemed to improve, however, when a letter from Lord Bellomont arrived. Bellomont, a devious fellow, promised to support Kidd's claim if the harried captain was able to produce the French papers that supposedly belonged to the *Quedagh Merchant*. With the good news, Kidd and his wife parted, never to be together again.

Anxious to clear his name, Kidd naively went to Boston to present his evidence to Bellomont, who was waiting to spring his trap. Only hours after arriving in Boston, Kidd was arrested, thrown into jail, and put in shackles. The trap was closing in on him, and all Bellomont needed was the *Quedagh*'s papers to have Kidd just where he wanted him.

Trapped like a mouse, Kidd panicked. Instead of realizing that Bellomont was orchestrating his doom, he stupidly handed over the only proof for his case to the scheming politician. Bellomont, concerned with protecting himself and the Whig politicians back in England, made the papers "disappear." Now Kidd had no proof for his defense; Bellomont's trap was shut tight, enabling the Whigs to use Kidd as a political scapegoat.

In 1700, the colonies were not authorized to try piracy, so Kidd was shipped back to London to face trial. Although Kidd professed innocence until the very end, Bellomont never came forward with the papers that would help his case. Without any evidence and also without a lawyer, Kidd didn't stand a chance. In 1701, Kidd was convicted on five counts of piracy and the murder of William Moore—the sentence was death by hanging.

On May 23, 1701, Kidd was loaded onto a cart and hauled to the gallows. The crowd that followed him was rowdy and drunk; public executions doubled as carnivals in eighteenth-century England. The crowd definitely got a show on that bizarre day: when Kidd's neck was put in the noose and the trap door opened, the rope, not Kidd's neck, snapped. Crashing to the ground, Kidd climbed the gallows again and was hanged a second time. This time the rope held and Kidd dangled until his unlucky spirit left his body.

The man who had been honored for his public service a mere decade before was now used as a warning to all would-be pirates. His body was tarred (a means of preserving flesh) and moved farther down the Thames River, where it hung in chains until it rotted away.

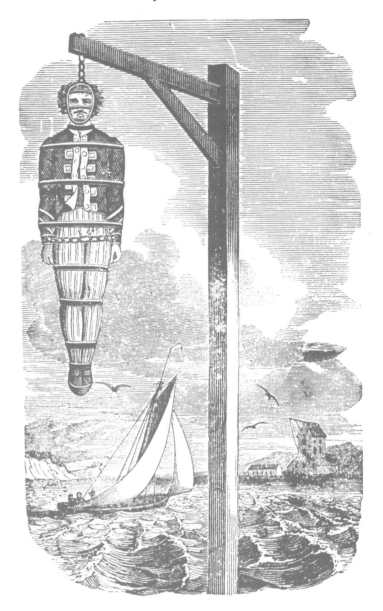

One hundred years after Kidd was hanged, the missing papers of the *Quedagh Merchant* were found in a government desk.

3

BLACKBEARD

IN THE EARLY 1700s, THE PIRATE HAUNT of new Providence Island in the Bahamas spawned a pirate whose very name sent chills down the spine of anyone hearing it: Blackbeard. A ferocious, blood-thirsty villain, Blackbeard worked hard to earn his nefarious reputation. His real name was Edward Teach, and his early life remains some-what of an enigma; some say he was born in Port Royal, Jamaica, while others contend his birth-place was Bristol, England. Despite the confusion, all agree that Teach was a poorly educated chap who first made a name for himself as a young English privateer in 1713. But within three years, Teach was better known as the infamous Blackbeard, ravaging the Bahamas and the American colonies until late in 1718.

Teach's pirate career began after his privateering career ended in 1714. Set-tling on New Providence Island, he fell in with Captain Hornigold, the leader of a cut-throat pirate squadron. Hornigold personally trained Teach in the art of piracy, treating him like his own son. Teach blossomed under Hornigold's guid-ance, demonstrating such a knack for piratical tactics that Horni-gold rewarded his star pupil with the command of a ship, which Teach named the *Queen Anne's Revenge*.

Not long after Teach acquired the *Queen Anne's Revenge*, Horni-gold, much to Teach's disgust, ac-cepted a Royal Pardon, a general amnesty for all pirates who agreed to give up their way of life. In 1716, Teach, feeling angry and betrayed by his mentor, swore that he would never give up "the sweet trade" of piracy. Ignoring the pardon, Teach, who now preferred to be called Blackbeard, raised the anchor and the Jol-ly Roger, setting off on a savage campaign in the Bahamas and North America.

Standing six feet four inches (190cm) tall and packing nearly two hundred fifty pounds (113kg) on his mammoth frame, Blackbeard was a mountain of a man capable of striking fear into any opponent—especially considering the fact that men of his time rarely reached even six feet (180cm). In battle, Blackbeard could keep his cutlass whirling long after most men were totally exhausted. He was also fond of the pistol, strapping as many as seven or eight to his body and firing point-blank at his opponents' chests or faces. Armed to the teeth, Blackbeard prepared for battle by adding gunpowder to a mug of rum, lighting the mixture, and then gulping the flaming drink. Fueled with this fiery brew, he was a ferocious warrior.

In addition to his mastery of conventional weapons, Blackbeard's arsenal included a daunting psychological

Above, left and right: Like Blackbeard, many pirates had a special fondness for their weapons. Pirates always kept their weapons in perfect working order. Failure to do so was a punishable offense.

weapon: the long, black beard from which his nickname derives. As coarse as steel wool, the legendary beard fell all the way to his waist. For added effect, he would braid the beard, tying colorful ribbons throughout. In battle, the ribbons were replaced by slow-burning gunner's matches, which when lit, made Blackbeard glow like a demon straight from hell. Daniel Defoe, inspired by the image of this flaming beard, wrote: "This beard, like a frightful meteor, covered his whole face, and frightened America more than any comet that has appeared there for a long time." The fiery beard undoubtedly added to the widespread speculation that Blackbeard either had a pact with the Devil or was Satan incarnate.

Blackbeard's peculiar behavior in battle was equalled by his quirky private life. A highly unstable character prone to unpredictable and bizarre impulses, Blackbeard kept his crew almost as frightened as their victims. On one occasion of relative calm, Blackbeard, being bored, invited two crewmen to join him for a drink around a candle-lit table. While they were seated around the table, he drew two pistols, blew out the candle, crossed his hands under the table, and discharged his weapons. One shot missed, but the other shattered the knee of his first mate, Israel Hands, laming him for life. When asked why he shot Hands, Blackbeard is reported to have

Blackbeard's crew carousing on the coast of Carolina.

answered: "If I did not now and then kill one of you, you'll forget who I am."

Fascinated with death—perhaps because he knew that his dangerous life-style destined him for an early grave—Blackbeard toyed with suidical and homicidal games. One day he shouted to his crew: "Come, let's make a hell of our own, and try how long we can bear it." Rushing below deck, Blackbeard and three crewmen battened down the hatches and lit several large pots of sulfur, which spewed out a foul, suffocating smoke. While the three men nearly choked to death before they burst onto the deck, Blackbeard danced and laughed, remaining in the smoke for several minutes longer. After enduring the smoke for an inhuman amount of time, he emerged from below looking as pale as a ghost.

One crewman gasped, "Why Captain, you look as if you were coming straight from the gallows!"

"My lad," he replied, "that's a brilliant idea. Next time we shall play at gallows and see who can swing the longest without being choked."

A truly morbid and freewheeling spirit, Blackbeard was also completely resistant to all attempts to reform him, especially those of his fourteen wives. Changing wives almost as often as he captured ships, Blackbeard enjoyed watching his wife-of-the-day dance, helping her along with carefully aimed pistol shots at her feet. When he grew bored with one wife, he simply locked her away with his treasure, leaving her to starve to death, and went in search of a new bride.

Blackbeard's unpredictable streak was a perfect asset for his profession. His first independent efforts in the Bahamas were so successful that he accrued a fleet of six vessels and four hundred men by 1717. Success bred confidence, so Blackbeard and his fleet brazenly glided north, cruising along the western coast of Florida and grabbing prize after prize. However, as he headed for the colonies, Blackbeard grew tired of the cat-and-mouse game of high-seas piracy—he was thinking of changing his style.

When he reached Charleston, South Carolina, Blackbeard was so bored with the ease with which he could chase down the clumsy merchant ships that he tried a new approach. Dropping anchor just outside the harbor, Blackbeard, knowing that merchantmen would eventually try to enter or leave Charleston, waited for the ships to come to him. Within days, Blackbeard had captured nine ships and taken the crews as prisoners without even a serious battle. The very sight of his flowing beard was enough to scare the merchant crews to death; never had piracy been so easy.

A pirate attack on colonial Carolina. Pirates often paid tribute to corrupt Carolina governors for safe haven in Carolina ports.

The situation changed a few days later, however, when an outbreak of venereal disease threatened Blackbeard's fleet. Desperately in need of medical supplies to save many of his crew, Blackbeard sent a landing party ashore. Needless to say, he had no intention of paying for the supplies. Blackbeard promised the mayor of Charleston that he would execute all of the prisoners and burn all of the ships in port if anything happened to the landing party or if the supplies he needed were not delivered in a timely fashion. The mayor, unwilling to sacrifice innocent lives, satisfied Blackbeard's demands, sending the supplies back with the landing party.

Blackbeard immediately released the prisoners and triumphantly sailed off to Bath, North Carolina, where he intended to nurse his crew back to health and clean the hull of his ship. Although his name was by this time synonymous with "villain" throughout the colonies, Blackbeard had a spe-

cial, secret relationship with the governor of North Carolina, Charles Eden, that assured him that he would not come under attack. While Eden publicly proclaimed that the pirate had accepted a Royal Pardon, the truth was that Blackbeard had privately bribed the governor; Blackbeard granted Eden a percentage of his pirate business in exchange for sanctuary. Although citizens of North Carolina, South Carolina, and Virginia vociferously complained about Blackbeard's continuing depredations, Eden refused to do anything so long as Blackbeard shared the wealth.

Stunned at Eden's apparent sheepheadedness, hordes of disgruntled North Carolinians turned to Alexander Spotswood, governor of Virginia, hoping he would do something about the accursed Blackbeard. Disturbed to find out that Blackbeard had abandoned his fleet and entered the Ocracoke Inlet in the *Queen Anne's Revenge* with the intention of creating a pirate enclave, the citizens pressed Spotswood for action. Spotswood, a fervent pirate-hater, swore he would do everything in his power.

By chance, two Royal Navy warships, the *Lyme* and the *Pearl*, were patrolling Virginian waters at the time. The commander, Lieutenant Robert Maynard, knew that the warships were useless against Blackbeard so long as he remained in the Ocracoke Inlet; riddled with sandbars and extremely shallow water, the inlet was too treacherous for the heavy warships. Spotswood, eager to solve the problem, rigged up two lighter, more navigable sloops for Maynard and fifty-eight of his crew. Spotswood also offered a £100 reward for the capture of Blackbeard—dead or alive.

Setting off on November 17, 1718, Maynard arrived outside the Ocracoke Inlet by sundown of November 22. With night fast approaching, he decided to delay his attack until sunrise because the inlet would be too difficult to navigate in darkness.

Meanwhile Blackbeard, aware that two ships had anchored outside the inlet near nightfall, made a few halfhearted preparations for battle before drinking himself into a stupor. After a night of raging drunkenness, the glassy-eyed Blackbeard watched as Maynard's sloops clumsily entered the inlet at sunrise. Within minutes, both sloops had run onto a sandbar, totally paralyzing Maynard's attack.

Raising the Jolly Roger, Blackbeard moved alongside the beached sloops, shouting, "Damn you for villains, who are you? And from where do you come?" As Maynard's crew desperately threw everything overboard in an attempt to free the sloops from the sandbar, Maynard boldly hoisted the White

Charleston, Carolina, was a pirate haunt in colonial times.

Ensign of the Royal Navy, shouting back, "You may see by our colors we are no pirates!"

Furious at such a snide remark from a totally vulnerable captain, Blackbeard lit one of his famous drinks, took a swig, and screamed, "Damnation seize my soul if I give you quarter or take any from you!" Without an offer of quarter, the battle would be to the death.

Aiming four cannons at each sloop, Blackbeard started the battle with a ferocious broadside, totally obliterating one sloop and killing twenty of the crew. Maynard's ship was still intact, however, giving the crafty lieutenant time to lure Blackbeard into a trap.

Realizing Blackbeard could simply use his cannon to finish off his beached sloop, Maynard artfully manipulated Blackbeard into boarding his sloop for hand-to-hand combat.

Sending his entire crew below deck and giving them instructions not to come back up until he gave the signal, Maynard remained at the helm, daring Blackbeard to come aboard. Blackbeard, with his mind still blurry from the previous night's drinking, foolishly fell into the trap. Fully intending to personally cut Maynard to pieces, he was the first man to board the sloop. Once Blackbeard and his crew were on the deck, Maynard gave the signal and his whole crew burst out, surprising the pirate attackers. The pirates recovered, however, and the battle raged on, the deck becoming slippery with the blood of both sides.

As the battle wore on, Blackbeard and Maynard came face to face. Both men fired their pistols at close range, but Blackbeard's shot missed while Maynard's crashed into the pirate's chest. Expecting the giant pirate to fall, Maynard momentar-

Blackbeard only moments before his death.

To announce his victory to the citizens of Carolina, Maynard had Blackbeard's head mounted on the bowsprit of his ship.

Maynard was greeted as a hero upon his return to Carolina.

ily revelled in his victory. Blackbeard, however, was hardly even stunned by the gaping wound in his chest. To Maynard's horror, Blackbeard raised his cutlass and with a mighty swing snapped Maynard's blade in two. Weaponless, Maynard prepared for his death.

But just as Blackbeard swung at Maynard, an unknown sailor darted toward Blackbeard from behind, slicing his throat. Emitting a gargled scream, Blackbeard missed the mark, and Maynard's life was spared. As Maynard's crew pressed the attack, Blackbeard's life was nearing an end. After four more pistol blasts and at least twenty deep stab wounds, Blackbeard finally tumbled to the deck like a falling tree. With their fearless captain down, the rest of the pirates lost heart and surrendered. The surviving pirates were thrown in chains, and all of them eventually swung from the gallows.

Sailing for Bath, Maynard wanted to grandly announce his victory to the citizens of the Carolinas, so he cut off Blackbeard's head and spiked it to the bowsprit, with the magnicent beard blowing in the wind. After Bath, Maynard went on to Virginia, where he collected his reward from Alexander Spotswood.

Even after the secret alliance that had been made between Charles Eden and Blackbeard was exposed, Eden remained free because there was not enough evidence to support the charges. Though Blackbeard was in the grave, piracy still had a friend in North Carolina.

4
BARTHOLOMEW ROBERTS

CAPTAIN BARTHOLOMEW ROBERTS WAS A rather peculiar pirate. Born in 1682 near Haverfordwest, in Pembrokeshire, Wales, he grew up to be a tall, handsome, dark-complexioned sailor. A puritanical Sabbatarian, he disliked liquor, preferring to drink tea, and insisted that the Sabbath be strictly observed on board his ships; even the musicians, who normally could be called upon to perform any hour of the day or night, were allowed to rest. He prohibited gambling and promised to kill any man caught trying to sneak a woman on board. A religious man, Roberts went into battle with a gold, diamond-encrusted cross dangling from his neck and, on one occasion, became so concerned with his crew's spiritual well-being that he tried to force a clergyman to minister the ship. With all of these traits and idiosyncrasies, Roberts would seem to be the most unlikely candidate for piracy. But what is most unusual about Bartholomew Roberts is that he was not only a pirate, he was the most successful pirate of all time. In only three years, between 1719 and 1722, Roberts captured over four hundred ships, an unprecedented and unbroken record.

The true irony of Roberts' outrageous success is that, like Kidd, he never wanted to be a pirate in the first place. In November of 1719, the thirty-seven-year-old Roberts was an honest crewman on the *Princess*, a slave ship sailing from London to the Gold Coast of Africa to pick up a load of slaves from Annamabo. While loading the "black ivory"—as slaves were referred to—onto the ship, two pirate vessels, the *King James* and the *Royal Rover*, seized the *Princess*. The pirate captain was Howel Davis, a fellow Welshman who, by some accounts, forced Roberts to join his crew.

A reluctant newcomer to piracy, Roberts pragmatically made the best he could of a bad situation. He demonstrated solid thinking and fierce fighting, earning the respect of his new mates. Indeed, Roberts was so well-respected that when Howel Davis was struck down during an unsuccessful attack on Prince's Island (now Príncipe), there was talk of nominating Roberts for the job, despite the fact that he had been with the pirates for only about six weeks.

Embroiled in a hot succession debate, the crew was swayed by the words of pirate Henry Dennis, who said, "It is my advice that while we are sober, we pitch upon a man of courage, and skilled in navigation, one who by his counsel and bravery seems best able to defend this commonwealth...such a man I take Roberts to be." Much to the dismay of several veteran pirates, Roberts was voted into office and accepted the position, saying, "since I have dipped my hands in muddy water, and must be a pyrate, it is better being a commander than a common man." But one bitter pirate, Walter Kennedy, waited for revenge.

After the *King James* sprang several leaks, the entire crew and all of the cannons were transferred to the *Royal Rover*. Sitting low in the water, the *Rover* prepared for action. Roberts' first major decision was to avenge the death of Howel Davis. Sailing into the harbor at Prince's Island, Roberts bombarded the fort and then set homes and ships on fire, moves that were extremely popular with his new crew.

Sailing away from the smoldering Prince's Island, the crew unanimously voted to head for Brazil. Crossing the Atlantic, the pirates arrived at Bahia Harbor to discover an enormous fleet of armed Portuguese merchantmen preparing for departure. Roberts hardly even slowed down as he ordered his crew below deck and sped toward the fleet. Looking relatively harmless, Roberts came alongside one of the ships and then dropped his anchor. Hailing the Portuguese captain, Roberts invited him aboard for a chat; once the unsuspecting captain was on the *Rover*, Roberts explained to him that he would die a painful death unless he pointed out the fattest, richest merchantman of the fleet. Armed with this information, he put the frightened captain back on his ship, hoisted the anchor, and glided toward his prey.

After a short exchange, Roberts' crew boarded the rich merchantman and seized the helm. As the *Rover* and the Portuguese ship casually slipped out of the harbor, not one of the armed ships gave chase. Laughing at the stupidity and cowardliness of the fleet, the pirate crew turned their attention to splitting the booty and, since Roberts frowned upon excessive drinking on board, finding a place to celebrate.

Fittingly, the pirates anchored at Devil's Island for their revelry. While his crew was carousing on the island, Roberts learned of a supply ship sailing nearby and rashly set off in a small, poorly provisioned sloop, leaving the majority of his crew on the island. Unable to catch the supply ship, Roberts returned to Devil's Island to find that Walter Kennedy had absconded with the *Rover* and the Portuguese prize—Kennedy had taken his revenge. Roberts was left with an unimpressive sloop, a few score men, and hardly any supplies.

Heading for Barbados, Roberts attempted to rebuild his fallen career but met with stiff resistance from two Barbadian men-of-war. In a furious battle, Roberts' sloop was badly damaged and thirty-five men were killed. He escaped destruction by jettisoning the heavy guns in order to lighten the ship and limped off to the Grenadines to make repairs. But Roberts

A quiet view of Bahia Harbor forty years before Roberts' legendary attack on the Brazilian port.

would never forgive the Barbadians for the attempts that they had made to destroy him.

Unlucky in the warm waters of the Caribbean, Roberts and his crew opted to try northern waters and set their sights on Newfoundland. Although Roberts was unaware at the time, the decision to head north saved his life—hours after he left for Newfoundland, two Martinican men-of-war arrived. The governor of Martinique, irate at the failure of his ships, insisted that Roberts be captured and his reign ended, but the ships had lost the trail.

Arriving at Newfoundland in June 1720, Roberts barged into the harbor of Trepassey with trumpets blaring and the Jolly Roger flittering in the wind. The crews of the twenty-two ships anchored in the harbor hurried ashore when they saw the pirate ship coming. As if to announce to the world that Bartholomew Roberts had returned, Roberts plundered every ship, seized one ship for his own, and set the rest ablaze.

After the Trepassey coup, Roberts roamed the Atlantic, hitting the Caribbean and western Africa with equal vigor. After catching scores of prizes, he anchored his new ship, the *Royal Fortune*, off the island of Tobago in the West Indies to rest and resupply. At this point, Roberts learned about the two Martinican ships that had nearly nabbed him in the Grenadines. Flying into a rage, Roberts vowed revenge against the governor and sailed toward Martinique, hell-bent on punishing the islanders.

In mid-February of 1721, Roberts seized a Dutch ship at St. Lucia, but only after a bloody, four-hour-long battle. Now Roberts had the perfect tool for his revenge. Knowing that the Dutch slave ships hoisted a flag to signal they were ready to trade slaves for money, Roberts sailed along the coast of Martinique under the appropriate signal and then watched as the unwitting traders sailed out to meet him. After anchoring nearby, the eager traders rowed to Roberts' ship and climbed onto the deck. Roberts quickly relieved each and every trader of his cash and then tied them up on one of the rowboats, torching the remainder.

Roberts seethed with hatred toward the governors of Martinique and Barbados for their repeated efforts to capture him. He took the issue so personally that he created his own pirate flag with a depiction of himself standing on two skulls. Each skull had three letters underneath it: one had ABH (for "A Barbadian's Head"), the other AMH (for "A Martinican's Head"). The flag was meant as a personal warning to the people of both islands, reminding them of what might happen if they should ever be taken prisoner.

The governors of Martinique and Barbados sent out repeated expeditions against Roberts.

Quitting the West Indies, Roberts sailed to western Africa, reaching the Senegal River by the middle of 1721. The Senegal River was a busy trade route for the French, who had a monopoly on slaves, guns, and ivory, and two French warships guarded the mouth of the river. When Roberts' sloop was spotted, the Frenchmen, mistaking the ship for a merchantman and unaware that the dreaded pirate Roberts was on board, sailed out to meet the approaching sloop. When Roberts raised the infamous Jolly Roger, the Frenchmen were so frightened that they surrendered without a fight. Roberts kindly put the Frenchmen ashore and appropriated both warships, renaming one the *Ranger* and using the other as a store ship.

With his new ships, Roberts went to Sierra Leone, where he learned that two fifty-gun Royal Navy warships, the *Swallow* and the *Weymouth*, had been sent to protect the African coast from pirates. Although he did not think much of the news at that time, Roberts became more concerned a few months later when he learned from an intercepted letter that the *Swallow*, captained by Chalenor Ogle, was only a few days behind him. Consulting his crew, Roberts decided to make for the island of Annabono, but the prevailing winds steered the pirates to Cape Lopez, where they dropped anchor in late January 1722.

Meanwhile, Ogle was forced to halt his pursuit at Prince's Island in order to bury dozens of his crew who had died from

fever. The *Weymouth* had suffered even worse: when the ship left England there was a crew of 240, but, constantly having to replace crew members, by the end of the voyage the captain's logs listed 280 dead. Despite the setbacks, Ogle was determined to end Roberts' illustrious career. He set off in the *Swallow* and eventually caught up with Roberts on February 5, 1722, at Cape Lopez.

After spotting Roberts in the harbor, Ogle was forced to veer away to avoid a sandbank, a move that Roberts interpreted as a sign of fear. Roberts sent out his consort, the *Ranger*, to capture the frightened quarry. Realizing that his maneuver had been incorrectly interpreted, Ogle continued to play the role of a fleeing merchantman, luring the *Ranger* out of hearing range of Roberts. When the pirates gained on Ogle and raised the Jolly Roger, he slowed his ship and pretended to surrender. But when the *Ranger* came alongside to board, Ogle ordered the lower ports raised and delivered a shattering broadside blow to the pirate sloop. Although the pirates put up a valiant fight, even attempting to blow up their ship rather than let her be taken by the Royal Navy, they could not fend off Ogle's crew. The *Ranger* was taken and Ogle prepared for his next move.

Sailing the *Swallow* back to Cape Lopez, the place where Roberts was anchored (enjoying a hearty breakfast of salmagundi and totally unaware that the *Ranger* had been captured), Ogle zoomed in on his prey. At first, Roberts took little notice of the ship bearing down on him, but when he saw the Royal colors, he barked orders to raise anchor and unfurl the sails.

Impeccably dressed in a rich damask waistcoat and breeches, with a red feather stuck in his cap, Roberts hastily decided on a dangerous and desperate battle plan: speed toward the warship, receive its fire, blast his own cannon, and then cram the sails and dash out of the harbor. The plan might have worked, but just as the sails were unfurled, the drunken crew was unable to catch the wind. Ogle came in for another broadside and Roberts was struck in the neck by grapeshot. Slumped on the deck, he appeared to his crew to be only wounded, but when a crewman rolled Roberts over, the horrible wound was exposed and all knew that Roberts was dead.

Once their leader was down, the pirates put up a feeble resistance. Captain Ogle took control of the ship, and most of the pirates were later hanged. Ogle was knighted for ridding the Atlantic of "the great pirate Roberts." With Roberts' death, a great chapter was closed in the golden age of piracy.

Bartholomew Roberts with the *Royal Fortune* and the *Ranger* at Whydah, a slaving port on the west coast of Africa. Eleven slave ships seized by Roberts in 1722 can be seen in the background.

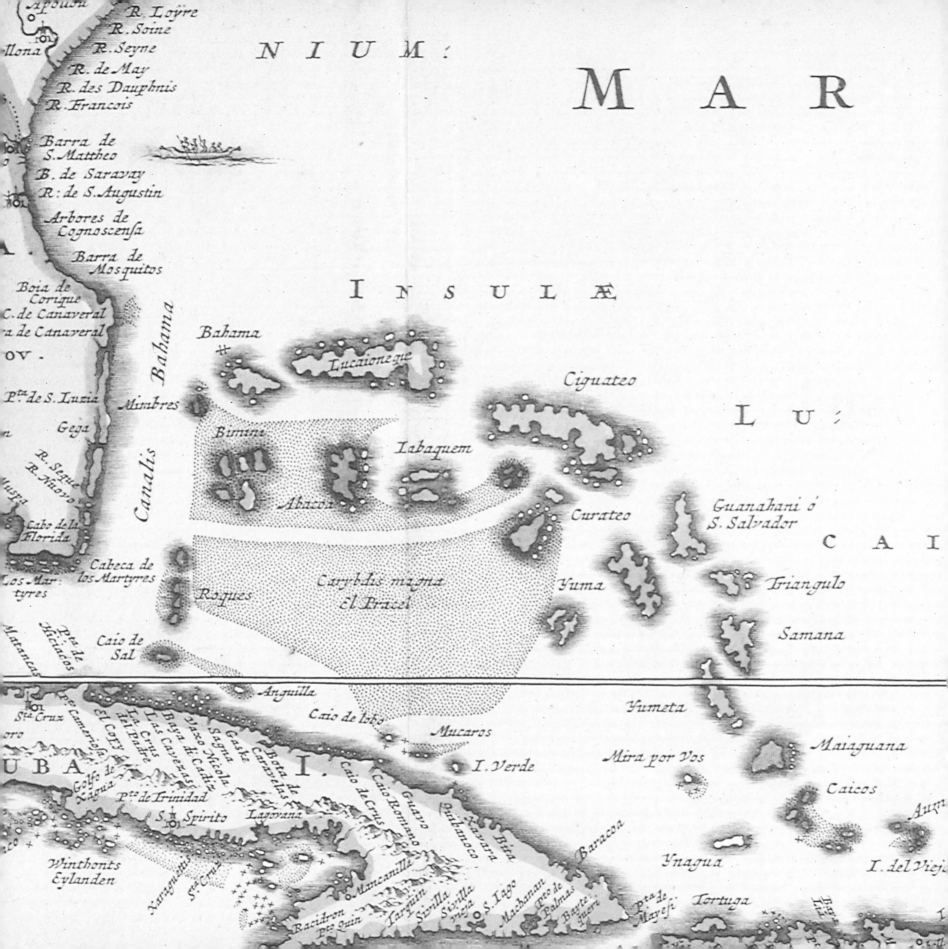

NIUM:

MAR

INSULÆ

LU:

CAI

R. Loyre
R. Soine
R. Seyne
R. de May
R. des Dauphnis
R. Francois

Barra de
S. Mattheo
B. de Saravay
R: de S. Augustin
Arbores de
Cognoscensa
Barra de
Mosquitos
Boia de
Corique
C. de Canaveral
ra de Canaveral
OV.
P.ta de S. Luzia
Gega
R. Seque
R. Nuovo

Cabo de la
Florida

Los Mar:
tyres
Cabeca de
los Martyres
Matanca

P.ta de
Hiciacos
Caio de
Sal

Bahama

Canalis

Mimbres

Bimini

Bahama

Lucaione que

Abacon

Roques

Ciguateo

Iabaquem

Curateo

Yuma

Carybdis magna
El Pracel

Guanahani ó
S. Salvador

Triangulo

Samana

Anguilla

Caio de Isbo

Mucaros

I. Verde

Yumeta

Mira por Vos

Maiaguana

Caicos

St Cruz

P.ta Cameriola
El Cosy
La Cruz
El Padre
Las Cabezas
Baya de Cadix
Baxo Nicola
Sagna
Gaske
Bota
Caravelas

P.ta de Trinidad
S. Spirito
Lagovana

UBA
I.
Golfo de
Xagua
Caio de Crus
Caio Borriano
Guavo
Quibanoco
Navara
Bira
Baracoa

Au
Ynagua
I. del Viejo

Winthonts
Eylanden
Xaragnatos
S.ta Cruz
Racitron
P.to quin
Yarquin
Mancanilla
P.to de
Quin
Sivilla
vieja
Machanan
S. Iago
P.to de
Palmas
Bayte
Jucri
P.ta de
Mayesi
Tortuga

5

MARY READ & ANNE BONNY

JACK RACKHAM, NICKNAMED "CALICO JACK" because of his fondness for calico underclothing, was a modestly successful pirate whose reputation and notoriety blossomed only after his capture. Rackham's piratical exploits in the Bahamas were impressive, but not nearly as impressive as the amazing story that unfolded once he and his unusual crew were taken into custody and put on trial.

Rackham's last day of freedom was a crisp, clear November day in 1720. Flushed with their recent success in the Bahamas, Rackham and his crew dropped anchor at Negril Point, located off the west coast of Jamaica, and brought out the rum for the requisite drunken celebration. In the midst of the celebration, a sloop was sighted in the distance, heading straight for the pirates. Knowing full well that the sloop was most likely commanded by Captain Jonathan Barnet, a brilliant bounty hunter who had been relentlessly pursuing the pirates for weeks, the crew threw their drinks overboard, unfurled the sails, and made a run for it.

Barnet, eager to collect the £200 bounty on Rackham's head, steadily gained on his quarry, finally coming within hailing distance near nightfall. Poised for the attack, Barnet offered Rackham and his crew a last chance to surrender, but Rackham defiantly responded by opening fire on his pursuer.

The ensuing battle was short and bloody. Rackham was totally outmatched as Barnet, a more skilled tactician, quickly outmaneuvered the pirate sloop and came in close enough for his crew to toss grappling hooks over the gunwales. As Barnet's crew swarmed the pirate deck, all but two of the half-drunk pirates panicked, scurrying below deck in a vain attempt to escape; the dashing Calico Jack turned tail and joined his mates below deck.

Mary Read

Anne Bonny, Mary Read, and friend try to stave off bounty hunters. Read became so enraged with her cowardly comrades that she shot one of them as he went below deck.

However, the two stalwart pirates who remained on deck carried on the fight with bravado. Shoulder to shoulder, the pair bravely stood their ground, growing so angry with their cowardly mates that one shot down into the hatch, killing one man and wounding another. But no matter how gallantly the pair raged on, two pirates were no match for an entire crew; the duo, overwhelmed by sheer numbers, surrendered.

With the surrender of the two fierce fighters, the battle was over, the ship secured, and Rackham dragged from below deck and slapped in chains. Rackham would then have become just another second-rate pirate destined for the gallows were it not for a startling revelation. When Rackham was put on trial at the Admiralty Court at St. Jago de la Vega, an unbelievable discovery was made—the two pirates who had fought like demons, the two savages who had stood their ground while their mates turned yellow, were not men, but women disguised as men! Mary Read and Anne Bonny were their names, and their unique story, which involved an unusual love triangle with Rackham, elevated all three pirates to celebrity status.

The Admiralty Court was stunned when the women revealed their true identities. That a woman would become a pirate was unusual enough, but that two women could end up walking the deck of the same ship, unaware for a long period of time of each other's identity, was absolutely astounding. When the story emerged, many could not believe the tale, but as the witnesses and evidence poured in, the undeniable truth was there for all to see.

Mary Read had never known her father, a sailor who had died at sea when she was still in her mother's womb. Read's mother, without a husband and already struggling to raise her other child, a boy, amidst the urban squalor of London, decided that the country would be a better place to raise her unborn child. Packing up her few possessions, she and her son moved to the country, where her daughter, Mary, was born not long after.

For four years, the family struggled to survive, but the country was no kinder to them than the city. At her wit's end, Mary's mother headed back to London, hoping that her deceased husband's mother, a successful businesswoman, would help support her grandchildren; the grandmother was known to cherish little boys and would probably help them out. There was only one problem: Mary's grandmother absolutely despised little girls.

Trudging back to London, Mary's mother had not figured out how to deal with her mother-in-law's foul disposition toward girls until fate played a hand. The tragic death of her son gave her a crazy idea. Dressing Mary in her dead brother's clothes, she trained her to talk and act like a boy, hoping to fool the grandmother when they arrived in London.

The scheme worked perfectly—almost too perfectly. Dodging the grandmother's original offer of room and board, a situation that would have undoubtedly led to the discovery of Mary's real sex, her mother instead worked out a weekly allowance for the support of the "lad" in another part of London. For many years, Mary was forced to maintain her false identity in order to keep the allowance on which she and her mother survived.

When Mary was thirteen, however, her grandmother passed away, and the allowance stopped. Read, by this time accustomed to life as a boy, decided that she had more of a future as a man than as a woman. With little future in London, she joined the Royal Navy, which did not bother to give the healthy new recruit a physical.

Read's first stint at sea was a short one; she tired of navy life quickly, deserted, and crossed the English Channel to Belgium, where she enlisted as a soldier in the British Army. One day a handsome young man was assigned to share quarters with Read, and she instantly fell in love with the strapping soldier. Acting like a star-crossed lover, Read allowed her military performance to fall to pieces; she failed to perform even the most basic of military duties and insisted on accompanying her bunkmate wherever he went.

Unable to contain her feelings, Read finally professed her love to the soldier, exposing her body to prove her womanhood. Thunderstruck at first, he soon returned Read's love, and they decided to marry. After announcing her identity and the marriage to the entire troop, she and her husband received honorable discharges and entered civilian life as man and wife.

But like her mother, Read was destined for a short married life. The couple opened up a successful tavern called The Three Horseshoes, but Read's husband died suddenly thereafter. Unable to run the tavern by herself, the heartbroken Read was forced to shut down the tavern and once again donned men's clothing to pursue a life of action.

Returning to life at sea, Read joined a Dutch merchantman bound for the Caribbean. En route, the Dutch ship was captured and plundered by English pirates. The captain, none other than Jack Rackham, offered Read, whose disguise was perfect, a position in his pirate crew because she was the only prisoner who spoke English. Read accepted, unwittingly becoming the second disguised woman on board; Anne Bonny was already sailing with Calico Jack.

Like Mary Read, Anne Bonny had begun to wear men's clothing because of a complex family situation. Bonny's father, an attorney in County Cork, Ireland, had been involved in a long-standing extramarital affair with his housemaid; the lawyer's wife, who at the time was spending a great deal of time away from home, suspected that her husband was sharing the housemaid's bed. To catch her husband in the act, the wife secretly returned home, sent the housemaid away, and awaited nightfall in the housemaid's bed. Events unfolded as she expected. "The husband came to bed, and that night play'd the vigorous lover, but one thing spoiled the diversion on the wife's side, which was, the reflection that it was not design'd for her; however she was very passive, and bore it like a Christian."

The pair separated soon after the incident, but the wife was forgiving enough to offer to pay for her husband's living expenses. Meanwhile, the husband and his mistress moved in together, and not long after, Anne was born. But afraid that Anne's presence would cause the wife to cut off support, Anne's parents dressed her as a boy, claiming that "he" was a distant nephew. The wife, doubting the story, conducted a secret investigation that revealed the true identity of the child. She was so outraged that she not only stopped supporting her husband, she was also successful in swinging public opinion against him.

Read and Bonny enjoy a quiet moment together. The two women became close friends after they learned each other's secrets.

As Anne's father's law practice collapsed after the embarrassing public scandal, the ostracized couple decided to emigrate to North America, where they could start a new life. Settling in Carolina, the lawyer became a successful plantation owner and watched as his daughter, now wearing the appropriate clothes, developed into a feisty, strong-willed, hot-tempered young woman. On one occasion, Anne grew so enraged with the improper advances of a suitor that she violently attacked him—the poor chap spent several weeks in bed recuperating from the flogging.

Anne, seeking a more rugged type of man than the plantation was able to provide, disguised herself in men's clothing and frequented the waterfront taverns and docks. Here she met a low-life seaman named John Bonny, whom she married without informing her father.

Anne Bonny, disowned by her father for her hasty wedding, set off with her new husband for the pirate enclave of New Providence Island. Once the couple reached the island, however, the marriage began to fall apart. John could not control his free-spirited wife, and she could not help questioning her husband's manliness.

As fate would have it, Jack Rackham, a novice pirate down on his luck, decided to accept a Royal Pardon and try civilian life on New Providence. Anne Bonny and Rackham met at a tavern, and they instantly knew that they were kindred spirits destined for a life of bold adventure. Rackham longed to return to piracy on the blue waters of the Bahamas, but he would only take Bonny with him on one condition: she would have to wear men's clothes and keep her identity a secret. Bonny readily agreed and left John without obtaining a legal separation.

Rackham, eyeing a speedy sloop anchored in the harbor, called on his old cronies while Bonny gathered information. The eager gang assembled on a dark and rainy night and stealthily rowed a small boat toward the anchored sloop. Swarming over the gunwales with Bonny in the lead, the pirates quickly seized control of the vessel. In the dark of night, the pirates easily glided past the harbor's fort and guardship, sailing off into the blue waters of the Bahamas and the pages of history.

Anne Bonny earned her keep on board the pirate sloop and was brutally effective in battle. She also shared the captain's bed. Through many battles and celebrations, the lovers kept their secret from the crew—until Mary Read was captured, joined the crew, and drove a wedge between them.

Bonny took an instant liking to Read, whom she took for a handsome sailor. Bonny and Read grew close, chatting away

Read, a fine swordsman who had served in the army, fatally wounds the man who had challenged her frail lover.

before battles and always fighting side by side. In time, Bonny's affections for the new pirate became more amorous, so she decided to reveal her true identity—only to find that Read herself was hiding the same secret. Although the revelation killed the budding romance, they both agreed to keep each other's secret. Rackham, however, growing jealous of Bonny's interest in the new seaman, promised to cut the latter's throat if the affair continued. To dispel Rackham's jealous rage, Read was compelled to reveal her identity to the captain, a secret which he kept from the rest of the crew.

Read's love life had one last chapter before her capture: she fell in love with a skinny, soft-spoken navigator who was forced into duty with the pirates after his ship was seized. She revealed her breasts to prove her sex, after which the navigator returned Read's love, and the couple remained wildly happy until a nasty turn of events.

Although the mild-mannered navigator was generally well-liked, one gruff mountain of a pirate gained pleasure from badgering him. One day when the navigator could take no more, he told the huge pirate what he really thought of him. The pair almost came to blows, but since fighting on board was a serious offense, they agreed to settle the matter by sword and pistol on dry land.

When Read learned about the impending duel, she was afraid for her lover's life. She knew that he was no match for the battle-tried pirate—even she would be hard-pressed to defeat him. The impending duel haunted Read's dreams until she came up with a plan. Strolling up to her lover's opponent, Read hurled insult after insult at him until the pirate challenged her

Ann Bonny *and* Mary Read *convicted of Piracy Nov.* 28*th* 1720 *at a Court of Vice Admiralty held at* S*t* Jago de la Vega *in y* Island of Jamaica.*

to a duel. Agreeing to a fight to the death, she scheduled her confrontation for two hours before her lover's appointed time.

When Read and her foe touched dry land, they fought for nearly two hours, trading blow after blow until Read finally ran her blade through the pirate. Just as he crumpled to the ground, the navigator arrived for his scheduled duel—only to find Read standing over the dead pirate with a smile on her face.

Returning to sea, the happy couple continued their affair, but their days were numbered. Rackham recklessly marauded the Bahamas, attracting the attention of the authorities, and only narrowly escaped several near captures. Fate finally caught up with Rackham and his crew when they were taken

prisoner in November 1720 at Negril Point. Jack Rackham and his female pirates would never sail together again.

Rackham was tried before Bonny and Read and was convicted of robbery on the high seas. Not long after Rackham's body was dangling from a rope, the unsympathetic Bonny had this to say: "If he had fought like a man, he need not have died like a dog." Bonny and Read were both convicted and sentenced to death, but the ladies pleaded for mercy, both claiming to be pregnant. Once their claims were verified, the executions were stayed.

Anne Bonny's fate remains a mystery: she was never heard of again. Mary Read died an unglamourous death during labor and was buried on April 28, 1721.

EPILOGUE

MOST PEOPLE BELIEVE THAT PIRATES ARE A PART OF the past. This is not true. On average, at least 120 ships are seized by modern-day pirates each year—and that does not include unreported incidents. Today, these desperadoes of the high seas use sophisticated technology like high-speed motor boats and radar to snatch cargoes worth extremely large sums of money. While the pirates of two centuries ago measured their loot in yards of silk and pigs of silver, today's pirates measure their success in tons of concrete, steel, coffee, car batteries, or ladies' underwear; the stolen goods are fenced through crooked merchants, and the pirates make away with cash. Pirates have even made off with entire bulk carriers, killing the crews and forging papers with new names for the contraband. Oil tankers from Exxon, Shell, and Mobil have all recently been hit by pirates. Piracy costs maritime trade a large amount of money every year, but little is heard about the problem because many shipping companies are embarrassed to admit that they cannot protect their own ships.

The hot spot of today's pirate scene is Singapore, the busiest port in the world. Asian pirates, many part of organized criminal syndicates, haunt the Straits of Malacca, where 240 ships pass through each day—one ship every six minutes. Typically, the pirates strike off the stern of an unsuspecting ship between 1 A.M. and 6 A.M. Although most of the pirates usually empty the captain's safe and then disappear, they sometimes take their sweet time in going over the entire ship. For example, on April 15, 1991, twenty armed pirates boarded the Hai Hui I, a merchant vessel carrying electronic goods. The captain and crew were handcuffed and locked in a cubicle for four days, where they heard the sounds of another ship and a crane being operated. When the ordeal was over, four hundred tons (360t) of electronics had disappeared.

Asia is not the only area plagued with piracy. Other recent pirate prizes have included 3,000 tons (2,722t) of sugar en route from Italy to Lebanon; 3,000 tons (2,722t) of steel nabbed in the Philippine Islands; and 2,500 tons (2,268t) of tomato paste bound for Algeria from Greece. Pirates ply their craft wherever opportunity knocks.

In all likelihood, piracy will never be completely eradicated from the maritime world. The lure of easy money and high adventure will forever attract men and women from all walks of life.

Merchant vessels are still vulnerable to pirate attacks in the unpoliced Straits of Malacca.

BIBLIOGRAPHY

American Heritage. *Pirates of the Spanish Main.* New York: American Heritage Publishing Co., Inc., 1961.

Black, Clinton V. *Pirates of the West Indies.* Great Britain: Cambridge University Press, 1989.

Defoe, Daniel. *A General History of the Pyrates.* Columbia, S.C.: University of South Carolina Press, 1972 (First Edition, 1724).

Ellms, Charles. *The Pirate's Own Book.* 1837.

Farnham, Alan. ''Pirates.'' *Fortune Magazine.* July 15, 1991: 112–118.

Gosse, Philip. *The History of Piracy.* New York: Burt Franklin, 1968.

Gosse, Philip. *The Pirates' Who's Who.* New York: Burt Franklin, 1968.

Marrin, Albert. *The Sea Rovers: Pirates, Privateers, and Buccaneers.* New York: Atheneum, 1984.

Ormerod, Henry A. *Piracy in the Ancient World.* Totowa, N.J.: Rowman and Littlefield Publishers, 1978.

Pringle, Patrick. *Jolly Roger: The Story of the Great Age of Piracy.* New York: W.W. Norton and Company, Inc., 1953.

Pyle, Howard. *Howard Pyle's Book of Pirates.* New York: Harper & Row Publishers, 1949.

Ward, Ralph T. *Pirates in History.* Baltimore: York Press, 1974.

PHOTOGRAPHY & ILLUSTRATION CREDITS

INDEX